HOMEMAKERS WITHOUT
THE MEN

HOMEMAKERS WITHOUT THE MEN

ASSAM'S WIDOWS OF VIOLENCE

BY WASBIR HUSSAIN

Indialog Publications Pvt. Ltd

Published in April 2006

Indialog Publications Pvt. Ltd.
O - 22, Lajpat Nagar II
New Delhi - 110024
Ph.: 91-11-29839936/29830504
Fax: 91-11-29835221
www.indialog.co.in

Printed at Print Tech, New Delhi.

ISBN 81-87981-86-5

This work is the outcome of a media fellowship awarded to Wasbir Hussain in 2005, by Women in Security, Conflict Management and Peace (WISCOMP), an initiative of the Foundation for Universal Responsibility of His Holiness the Dalai Lama. It was initially published by WISCOMP as part of its ongoing series titled 'Discussion Papers' (Discussion Paper 8).

CONTENTS

PREFACE

In any conflict situation, women and children are directly or indirectly drawn into the vortex of the problem, and Assam, northeastern India's largest state, is no exception. There are innumerable instances of husbands, sons and brothers, besides women themselves, getting killed at the hands of either militants or of the security forces who battle the militants. In some cases, people have been shot dead by unidentified gunmen who pass off as "secret killers."

A large number of militant cadres belonging to the United Liberation Front of Asom (ULFA), the National Democratic Front of Boroland (NDFB) and other groups have been killed by security forces during anti-insurgency operations. Similarly, militants have killed many security personnel and ordinary civilians. Besides, hundreds of people have been killed in bloody ethnic wars, mostly over territorial supremacy, that take place in various parts of Assam at regular intervals. Thousands have been uprooted from their homes at different times.

This has led to a situation where scores of households

across Assam have come to be headed by women who have lost the breadwinners of their families, be they husbands, sons or brothers. Setting aside their own personal loss, these women often have to earn their livelihoods, sometimes for the first time in their lives. Widows of this kind of violence have to take care of the wellbeing and education of their children as single parents, and determinedly create a cheerful atmosphere in their homes, so that the children can successfully emerge from their trauma to some kind of normalcy. These women have been forced to run their families in the face of heavy odds. Indeed, these are remarkable women who have not given up on life.

Having written on insurgency and ethnic strife in Assam and elsewhere in northeastern India for the past two decades, I was very keen to study the lives of the widows of violence, to begin with in Assam. I was primarily interested in letting readers feel their sorrow, struggle, anguish and pain, and, of course, show how they faced life with the utmost courage and determination, and how they managed to overcome their problems. But the demanding nature of day-to-day reportage for an international wire service, writing a weekly column in a regional newspaper, and looking out for news and features for a leading national weekly magazine, had prevented me from executing my dream project.

Towards the end of 2004, I got into a "now-or-never" mood. I sent off a proposal, titling it 'Homemakers Without the Men,' to the New Delhi-based WISCOMP – Women in Security, Conflict Management and Peace, an initiative of His Holiness the Dalai Lama. WISCOMP accepted the proposal, and I was awarded a Scholar of Peace Fellowship. I am truly indebted to WISCOMP for accepting my proposal and letting me work on a subject that had always fascinated me.

By March 2005, I had shortlisted women survivors located in different parts of Assam. By April, I was out in the field driving through horrible roads and traversing rickety wooden bridges on certain occasions, and meeting them. Some of the areas I passed through were, not long ago, the battleground for rival ethnic militias. That was in the western Assam Bodo tribal heartland.

Marble or concrete memorials by the roadside, listing the names of the dead, were grim reminders of the mindless violence that the area had witnessed. That was a common sight in or around towns like Serfanguri, Banargaon and others in Kokrajhar district. Often, there would be people stopping by to take a look at these neat cenotaphs.

The Fellowship required that I publish a 12-part series on my theme in the print media. I chose *The Sentinel*, an English daily from Guwahati, due to my personal association with the paper as a Consulting Editor. At this point, I would like to thank Mr Shankar Rajkhewa, Director of *The Sentinel*, now the Editor, for showing a lot of interest in my work. My sincere thanks also go to the then Editor, Mr H.K.Deka, for readily agreeing to publish the series in the editorial pages that he supervised personally. Their interest in the series enthused me to go ahead with my project and finish it in just about eight months. That happened because my articles were slotted for every alternate Sunday.

Mr Deka said he was deeply moved by the stories of the women survivors and suggested that I should get the series published in the form of a book. That, however, depended on getting a publisher, but the idea did stick. When I discussed the idea with the Editors at Indialog Publications, they liked it almost immediately. My sincere thanks to Indialog Publications.

I am also indebted to many people who have helped me by way of identifying the women I eventually met and interviewed, and providing me with a great deal of detail about the events of the time. Ajit Basumatary and Jaiklong Brahma, two young journalists based in Kokrajhar, deserve special mention. They accompanied me through the remote, inaccessible places of western Assam's Kokrajhar district to meet some of the survivors. They had in fact visited some hamlets beforehand, in order to ensure that I could locate the women easily later. Iqbal Ahmed, a journalist in Dibrugarh in eastern Assam, took pains to locate some women among the names I had sent him.

A big thank you to Biju Boro, a dynamic photo journalist, who accompanied me on my trips. My thanks also go to the many people who have responded to my series. And, of course, a special thanks to a thinking police officer,

Bhaskar Jyoti Mahanta, IPS, and my college mate Gautam Bordoloi – I don't know if he still believes in Zen-style meditation – for their feedback after every story.

The list is long, and I apologize for not being able to specifically thank by name all those who helped me. But I cannot end without thanking my wife Seema who read every story and gave her critical comments. At times I agreed with her and made the necessary alterations. Thanks are also due to my daughter Nazia and son Farhan for not complaining, and waiting for answers to their innumerable questions on anything under the sun, as I could hardly give them time during the couple of months I was travelling or writing.

Here, then, are the stories of some of these indomitable women. I have written them as simply as possible, as plain narratives.

WASBIR HUSSAIN

ASSAM'S "LITTLE WARS": AN INTRODUCTION

If wars cause death and devastation, "little wars" too kill and maim. In a way, "little wars" – or "low intensity conflicts" as they are known in security parlance – are more disturbing, because they take place between two communities who have lived together in peace till one day a spark ignites and burns up the age old bond. "Little wars" are also fought between ethnic or separatist militants on the one hand, and government forces on the other. The results are the same: the death of loved ones, the misery of the survivors, the displacement of thousands and a deep mistrust and suspicion between two communities with the divide between them often becoming unbridgeable.

Assam has been witness to violent insurrections for separate homelands, armed campaigns by ragtag and bobtail rebel armies seeking either self-rule or maximum autonomy, and bloody feuds between ethnic groups over territorial supremacy. These "little wars" have made this state of 26 million people, stretching over 78,438 square kilometres, one of South Asia's hottest trouble spots, sucking into the vortex of the conflicts women, children and innumerable other innocent people. It is not surprising to find trouble in Assam, for the state, like the other northeastern Indian states, is an ethnic minefield, being home to diverse ethnic groups and communities.

THE RISE OF INSURGENCY

Rich in natural resources, Assam was a relatively peaceful state until the formation of the United Liberation Front of Asom (ULFA) on April 7, 1979. A group of six radical Assamese youths met that day at the Rang Ghar, the famous amphitheatre of the Ahom royalty (the Ahoms ruled Assam for 600 years, 1228 AD onwards), launched the ULFA and vowed to fight the Indian state until they achieved a "sovereign, socialist Assam." During that meeting in a corner of the two-storied red brick monument in the eastern district town of Sivasagar, they concluded that the people of Assam were being "exploited" by what they called "the colonial Indian government." The state's rich tea, oil and forest resources, the youths agreed, were being "exploited" by "outsiders" without much benefit to the locals. They resolved to fight for the rights of their people. The culture of violence had begun in the state.

By the mid-eighties, Assam was in the grip of the ULFA. Rebels belonging to the group killed, kidnapped and threatened tea planters and businessmen across the Brahmaputra river valley and generally created a reign of terror. The rebel group wanted funds to purchase military hardware and to send its cadres for advanced weapons training to Myanmar, Afghanistan and other places, and an element of terror was required to make people pay up. Among those assassinated by the ULFA was Surrendra Paul, chief of the Calcutta-based Apeejay Group of Industries that owns several tea plantations in Assam. Paul, who was shot dead during a visit near the eastern Assam district town of Tinsukia on April 9, 1990, was the brother of Indian-born British business tycoon Lord Swraj Paul.

The tea lobby was powerful. After all, the industry's annual turnover in Assam is put at more than Rs. 3,000 crores today. The planters' lobby exerted tremendous pressure on New Delhi to adopt some tough measures to rein in the ULFA. In a secret operation on November 8, 1990, a chartered aircraft landed in an abandoned airfield at Sookerating, near Tinsukia, 550 kilometres east of Guwahati, the capital of Assam, and evacuated around a dozen panic-stricken executives and their family members belonging to the multinational Unilever Group that had seven tea plantations in the area. These men had received threats from the ULFA.

This created a very bad image of the security situation in the state. New Delhi responded by dismissing the Assam Government, then headed by a regional party, the Asom Gana Parishad (AGP), with Prafulla Kumar Mahanta as Chief Minister. This happened on the night of November 27-28, 1990. Simultaneously, the Indian government launched the first-ever systematic counter-insurgency operation against the ULFA, code-named "Operation Bajrang." The Indian Army smashed the ULFA's Central Headquarters deep within the Lakhipathar jungles, near Tinsukia. The rebels were on the run and would engage in a hit-and-run bush war with the security forces for years to come.

Over the years, the ULFA grew in strength, established trans-border linkages with rebel groups both within the North East and in neighbouring Southeast Asian nations, and continued with its armed campaign for an independent Assam. By 1991, the ULFA was firmly ensconced in the adjoining Himalayan kingdom of Bhutan and operated from its bases there until the Bhutanese military launched an assault and expelled them in December 2003.

The ULFA insurgency certainly resulted in the proliferation of insurgent outfits in the state. Different ethnic groups like the Bodos, the Karbis and the Dimasas created their own militant organizations to push ahead with their demands, ranging from self-rule to maximum autonomy and independent homelands. The rise of ethnic militant groups such as the United People's Democratic Solidarity (UPDS) or the Dima Halam Daoga (DHD) resulted in violent clashes, with innocent civilians belonging to both communities being directly hit.

A radical section of the Bodo tribespeople in western Assam formed what was then called the Bodo Security Force (BSF) on October 3, 1986. This was at that time the only other militant group to have demonstrated its strike potential besides the ULFA. The BSF, which was later re-christened as the National Democratic Front of Boroland (NDFB), was engaged in a bloody campaign for an independent Bodo homeland. Exactly a decade later, on June 18, 1996, another Bodo militant group emerged on the scene, called the Bodo Liberation Tigers (BLT). Unlike the NDFB that was demanding an independent Bodo homeland, the BLT sought a separate state for the Bodos within India. Many Bodos, including cadres from both the rebel groups, were killed in vicious fratricidal battles.

On February 10, 2003, however, the curtain was drawn over the BLT insurgency with the rebel group signing an agreement with New Delhi. By the terms of this agreement, a 40-member elective politico-administrative structure with maximum autonomy, the Bodoland Territorial Council (BTC), came into being. Besides, three new districts were created. On May 25, 2005, however, the NDFB too, entered into a ceasefire agreement with the Government after the group responded favourably to the Chief Minister of Assam, Tarun Gogoi's September 30, 2004 call for truce, and has begun peace negotiations with the Indian Government.

Assam nevertheless has come to be known as an insurgency hotspot. In just one decade, 1992-2002, as many as 4,888 people have been killed across the state in insurgency-related violence. These included 643 personnel of security forces and 2,597 civilians. Besides, the number of people killed in ethnic flare-ups is estimated to run into several hundreds, although accurate statistics are not available. In fact, security agencies had, at one stage, identified as many as thirty five terrorist and insurgent groups, operating in different parts of Assam. Most of them have become defunct over the years, and many are just rag-tag entities without any proper ideology. Many have arrived at formal or informal understandings with the authorities and have since shunned violence, while those like the NDFB, the UPDS, the DHD and others, as mentioned above, have, in principle, decided to talk peace.

THE IDEA OF ETHNIC HOMELANDS: A RECIPE FOR TROUBLE

The Indian Government appears to have been convinced that an integrationist policy in holding the North East together was, after all, not a correct approach in view of the diverse nature of the region's demographic profile. This may have prevented it from performing its role as a "homogenizing State." Instead it recognized the uniqueness, the differences and distinct identities of the region's ethnic groups and communities.

It seems that it is this recognition that is behind the Indian Government's conceding to demands for autonomy time and again, making it give in to the aspirations of different ethnic groups at different points of time. This, in turn, has opened up a Pandora's box. There has been a proliferation of movements to achieve economic and political liberation on ethnic lines, thereby leading to feuds between ethnic groups over territorial supremacy within the region.

It seems that the idea of ethnic homelands has come to be deeply ingrained in the minds of the ethnic militants in Assam and elsewhere in northeastern India. If New Delhi and the state governments have also come to accord legitimacy to the aspirations of the ethnic groups by conceding, in some form or the other, to their demands for autonomy, the ethnic militants or their mainstream support groups appear to have concluded that they can achieve their goal if they can keep up their political mobilization. It is not entirely untrue that the Government has generally attached more importance to groups or militias that have a greater track record of violence than other assemblages representing the same ethnic group or community.

Another look at Bodo politics in Assam may be relevant here, since it shows just how an ethnic organization or militia's dream of a homeland does not end with the conceding of some autonomy to the community by the Government. If there is a relative calm in Assam's Bodo heartland today, it is because of the signing of the peace agreement with the Bodo Liberation Tigers on February 10, 2003. A total of 2,641 BLT rebels laid down arms on December 26, 2003. The agreement led to the BLT giving up its demand for a separate Bodo state within the country. Instead, a 40-member elective politico-administrative structure with maximum autonomy, the Bodoland Territorial Council, was created.

Another development led to more euphoria on the Bodo front. After some uncertainty, the predictable happened: the outlawed NDFB too signed a ceasefire agreement with the Government. The truce, inked in New Delhi on May 25, 2005, between the NDFB, the Union Government and the State Government of Assam, was for a year to begin with, and came into effect from June 1, 2005. The outfit, headed by Ranjan Daimari, aka D.R. Nabla, its "President," had, at that time, an estimated five hundred trained fighters according to intelligence estimates, although its overall cadre strength is said to be around two thousand.

Having made visible progress in their efforts to bring back peace to the state, both the Assam Government and the Union Government appeared happy. The stage was set for the beginning of a process of negotiation for permanent peace between the Government and the NDFB leadership. It is true that there have been several roadblocks that have prevented the formal NDFB-Government peace talks from taking off. It is a matter of time before the two sides sit across the table and work towards an "acceptable solution." But events that could follow from this point onwards promise to be highly unpredictable, if not downright dangerous.

What is absolutely unforeseeable is the possible shape of the deal with the NDFB and its fallout on Bodo politics, which has always been murky. What can the NDFB bargain for? A Union Territory for the Bodos, or a brand new autonomy package? Would that mean that New Delhi can or will scrap the agreement that it signed in 2003 with the Bodo Liberation Tigers to end that group's armed campaign for autonomy? Can there be a new Bodo accord without disturbing the one already in place, in accordance with which the Bodoland Territorial Council came into existence? No player in the tortuous Bodo political arena has a clue. The Central and State Governments also seem to have no game plan beyond the beginning of 2006.

As things stand, a new turf war is bound to emerge the moment an agreement between the Government and the NDFB takes shape. The war that has bloodied Assam's Bodo inhabited areas from the time the BLT emerged on the scene in 1996 could resurface in various forms once again. The NDFB and the BLT have been bitter foes, the former fighting for an independent homeland, and the latter, from the beginning, pushing for maximum autonomy for the Bodo ethnic group within the ambit of the Indian Constitution.

There is actually very little political space vacant now in the Bodo heartland, particularly since the BLT bid adieu to arms and joined the political and social mainstream after the agreement with New Delhi in 2003. The BTC has been created under the terms of the agreement, three new districts were carved out, an annual allocation of one billion rupees has been earmarked for the new Council, and former BLT cadres have been absorbed into the paramilitary forces as part of a rehabilitation package.

Significantly, while the major mainstream Bodo forces, including erstwhile BLT members, the All Bodo Students' Union and others had wholeheartedly backed the BLT-led autonomy campaign, they turned political rivals the moment the first elections to the BTC were announced. The BTC polls, held on May 13, 2005, witnessed former BLT "chief," Hagrama Mahilary, openly campaigning against official candidates nominated by the newly floated Bodo People's Progressive Front (BPPF). This, despite the fact that the BPPF had the backing, at least officially, of the ABSU and also the former BLT, and was a political party meant to accommodate all the pro-BLT forces, including the group's mainstream allies such as the ABSU and others.

But in less than six months after the maiden polls to the newly created BTC, its leaders were trying to outdo each other for the sake of political power. The nascent Bodoland People's Progressive Front will either split or is on the verge of a split because former BLT supremo Hagrama Mahilary is at loggerheads with the party president Rabiram Narzary. If the mainstream Bodo groups themselves cannot resolve their differences and present a united front, it is unrealistic to expect things to be smooth once the NDFB begins formal peace talks with New Delhi, reaches an agreement and is left to share power with the existing BLT-led political forces running the administration in the Bodo-dominated areas. The turf war then is bound to heat up.

Indications of trouble have already emerged. Hagrama Mahilary, while welcoming the NDFB-Government truce, has made it clear that New Delhi must look for a solution without disturbing the existing BTC. On his part, Assam Chief Minister Tarun Gogoi has said in no uncertain terms that there was no question of conceding to any demand for a separate Bodo state. If that continues to be the Government's position, the NDFB will have to be satisfied with another "autonomy package."

Whatever that may be, it will certainly have the potential to disturb the prevailing Bodo power equations. And the former BLT rebels could well be poised for a new turf war with the NDFB. There will, of course, also be other major political realignments, making the scene in Assam's Bodo heartland even more volatile.

There was a time when the influential ABSU used to call the shots insofar as mainstream Bodo politics was concerned. On this occasion, the ABSU did not succeed in patching up the differences – mainly the rift within the BPPF – within the Bodo political spectrum. For some time, however, at least until the talks with the NDFB reach a decisive stage, with all insurgent groups joining the peace bandwagon, a relative calm can be expected in the Bodo dominated areas. But the fissures within the mainstream Bodo groups can create a situation where newer radical forces may emerge and take control of things. In that case, the Bodo heartland will be plunged into fresh turmoil.

If at one time the Government's decision to include only those villages that had a fifty per cent Bodo population into the Bodoland Autonomous Council triggered off an ethnic cleansing of the Santhals, the compulsion to grant autonomy or even sign a new Bodo peace deal, this time with the NDFB, can actually keep the Bodos' dream of a homeland alive. In addition, having two separate autonomy agreements with outfits representing a single ethnic group can set a precedent. This can come in handy for other ethnic militias or mainstream ethnic organizations in Assam or elsewhere in northeastern India to keep pushing their homeland demands with periodic modifications. And conceding to these demands will always increase the possibility of more ethnic violence and ethnic cleansing.

COUNTER-INSURGENCY: QUESTIONABLE METHODS

The Government and security establishments in India would perhaps do well to get rid of the term "counter-insurgency" and describe drives against militancy as "anti-insurgency" operations instead. We can call a rebel an insurgent. But can we call a member of the police, army or the paramilitary deployed for anti-insurgency duties a counter-insurgent? No. Sadly states such as Assam have witnessed certain extra-constitutional acts such as the assassination of militants' kin or others by mystery men who have come to be popularly described by the media as "secret killers." In that sense, there existed, and still exists, counter-insurgents in Assam! In fact, the State Government, by instituting probes into a few deaths in the state by "secret killers," have confirmed the existence, at least at one time, of such mystery men out to teach the insurgents a lesson.

In some of the chapters of this book, I have written about widows such as Bharati Rajkonwari, wife of Dimba Rajkonwar, brother of ULFA chairman Arabinda Rajkhowa, and Bharati Kalita, sister of ULFA "Deputy Commander in Chief," Raju Baruah, whose husbands were shot dead by "secret killers" although they did not have direct links with the rebel group. Similarly, several members of ULFA publicity chief Mithinga Daimary's family were eliminated by "secret killers." The list is a long one. It is not known whether these people were killed by some overzealous men in uniform, or by militants who had surrendered to the Government. In any case, these "surrendered militants" have come to constitute a class in themselves in Assam. What is known, however, is that such killings have led to bloody revenge attacks, often directly affecting innocent people, further complicating the state's security scenario and lending a new twist to the dynamics of conflict.

Anti-insurgency operations in Assam have been going on for more than fifteen years now, from the night of November 27-28, 1990 to be precise, when "Operation Bajrang" was launched by the Army against the ULFA. And yet, insurgency or violence by armed groups continues. ULFA's growth may have been kept in check by the sustained military operations, but the rebel group has not really been marginalized. ULFA continues to be a potent force, changing strategy and resorting to deadly explosive attacks through much of 2003 and 2004. These attacks required just one or two cadres to devastate the earmarked area. ULFA's recruitment drives also continue.

If the Government has come forward to hold peace talks with the ULFA, it is largely because of the realization that the group cannot be eliminated through military operations. A political initiative to bring about a political solution was, therefore, undertaken, particularly after ULFA took the initiative in September 2005 to nominate an 11 member panel of "like-minded people" from Assam to start exploratory talks with New Delhi. The panel, which ULFA has called the People's Consultative Group (PCG), held the first round of talks in New Delhi in October 2005, with Prime Minister Manmohan Singh attending the inaugural session and sending out a clear message that the Indian Government was indeed serious in bringing peace back to Assam.

If the exploratory talks between the ULFA-nominated panel and New Delhi fail to achieve the desired result, that is, preparing the ground for direct talks between the ULFA and the Government, things could once again heat up in Assam. "Acceptance of the PCG's proposals will pave the way for peace talks and their rejection will make the struggle more vigorous," the ULFA has said in its mouthpiece Swadhinata ("Freedom") in the November 2005 issue. Now, if the talks are derailed, the ULFA could once again step up violence. That would lead to an intensified anti-insurgency operation. In that case, will "secret killers" or certain other extra-judicial forces come into play once again?

Going by precedence, one never knows.

BIRSA KUJUR:
A SURVIVOR OF THE BODO-SANTHAL BATTLE

It was a humid May afternoon in 2000 when I first met Birsa Kujur. Clad in a tattered shirt and a half lungi, this sixty year old Santhal tribal was having his meal. This consisted of nothing more than mashed wild potatoes. These tubers, collected from the jungles, need to be soaked overnight in water before they are fit for consumption, and some of them can even be poisonous. Kujur was aware of the dangers, but he had no choice. He was weak and infirm. His wife had one day been bitten by a snake while she was out looking for these wild tubers. She survived. There had been occasions when Kujur and his wife had had to make a meal of rats. These are not easy to get either. They had to hunt for them, painstakingly smoking the creatures out of their holes.

Kujur was among the 17,000 inmates at the Joypur Relief Camp, located by the highway in Western Assam's Kokrajhar district, around 250 kilometres from Guwahati, the capital city. The highway, in fact, links Assam and the rest of the northeastern states to the Indian mainland through Siliguri, in West Bengal. The camp was set up by the authorities to shelter the displaced Adivasi Santhals following the bloody ethnic riots in 1996 between the community and the Bodo tribespeople who form the majority in the area. There were other such camps in the neighbourhood that sheltered Bodos who had been hit by the clashes, although not to the extent, perhaps, as the Santhals had been.

These settlements were relief camps only in name. Kujur and the others had to live in tiny reed-walled hutments, with roofs of plastic sheeting, without any sanitation or healthcare facilities, in almost sub-human conditions. In February 2000, the inmates of the camp received government rations for only ten days. Besides, 620 gms and 400 gms of rice for each adult and child respectively per day and about 50 gms of salt per person was hardly enough even for people who are supposed to live on just two meals a day. In March, rice was again provided for only ten days. And in April 2000, the people living in the camp had to make do with the rice supplied to them for just five days. If Kujur and his wife had to hunt for wild tubers, others like Phagu Lakra had to set out every morning with their axes and other iron implements to dig out the stumps of trees – felled illegally in the past – to cut them into pieces and sell them to buyers along the highway. After all, every rupee was important.

"Despite the living conditions, we feel safe here. At least the children can sleep without being constantly afraid of armed raiders descending on their village homes at night," said Robin Hembrom, then a 26-year-old Adivasi student leader. Many of the children showed signs of post-traumatic stress. After all, the riots had indeed been blistering. More than 300,000 people belonging to both communities were displaced, and nearly 250 people were killed in the bloodshed that began on May 15, 1996 and continued sporadically till the end of that year. Another 200 people died when the Bodos and the Santhals battled again in 1998.

Life, of course, had to go on. The small signboard at the entrance to the camp proclaimed that the long thatch-roofed barrack was a school. It was the Joypur Relief Memorial School set up in 1996 with the help of the Lutheran World

Service (LWS). In fact, the Christian missionaries belonging to the LWS were almost the only personnel from non-governmental organisations who provided relief to these hapless people during the initial days. The school had about 1,000 students. "Six of our students have appeared for the school final examinations this year," said Raghunath Tudu, who was the headmaster then. Tudu himself studied only till the twelfth standard. There were thirteen teachers, all of whom lived in the camp itself.

From one of the by-lanes in the settlement emerged four drummers in full flow. A day after they had performed at a wedding, they were still on the job. Baha Murmu, a girl from the camp had married a boy from the nearby Simorgaon Adivasi settlement. "We served the groom's party red tea and puffed rice," said Sonamoni Murmu, a relative. I saw a weaving centre, a church, three temples, a barber's shop and a small market within the camp. It presented a picture of people coming to terms with reality, a picture that showed no signs of change for the better.

I left the place and drove to the Amguri relief camp, closer to Kokrajhar, the headquarters of the district. This camp had Bodo and Rabha tribals and was "adopted" by the Army's 18 Field Regiment in October 1998. This was a smaller place and had about 1,100 inmates living in 179 thatch hutments. It was the same story here. Rations for five days in April, no doctors, no medicines. Boloram Narzary, 70, one of the refugees, was livid. "Do the government babus expect us to eat for five days and then go hungry for the rest of the month? It is better to die than live such a life."

Why weren't they returning to their village homes? Narzary, a Bodo tribal, had the answer: "We were living in peace with the Santhals. But now, after the riots, we cannot trust them." Unlike the inmates of the Joypur camp who had nowhere to return to as most of them were illegal encroachers in forest reserves, the refugees at Amguri were from five villages – Mainaguri, Samaguri, Bolomguri, Dumbruguri I and Dumbruguri II. The people would go to their villages to cultivate their land during the day and return by nightfall to the camp. At this camp too, there were schools – four in all.

Both communities, the Bodos and the Santhals, had been living in peace in the area for decades. The Bodos are the largest of the "Plains Tribes" of Assam and live primarily along the northern banks of the Brahmaputra river. The Bodo population was estimated at 1.2 million in 1991. This is "an ethnic group of people belonging to the great Mongoloid stock…. the Bodos claim that they are the first comers (to the Assam plains) and therefore they demand a better share of the land." The movement of populations resulted in the relative political marginalization of this numerically dominant tribe, making them restive, to put it mildly.

Things soon took a violent turn. After the first Bodo Accord of 1993, signed between the All Bodo Students'

Union (ABSU, the apex student group of the Bodos) and its allies, and the Government of India, the Government came up with a formula through which only those villages with a 50 per cent Bodo population were to be included in the newly created Bodoland Autonomous Council (BAC). This provision was generally believed to have encouraged a section of Bodos, including armed militant groups claiming to represent the community, to attempt ethnic cleansing. They began to drive out the non-Bodos in order to convert vast stretches into Bodo majority areas and thereby get them included in the BAC and widen its territory.

The minority Santhals, living in some large pockets within the area, were the worst affected. The radical elements within the Santhal population responded by forming rag-tag armed groups with belligerent names such as the Adivasi Cobra Militants of Assam. The Cobra rebels began by snatching arms from the police and the paramilitary troopers, and had the potential to transform themselves into a more organized militant outfit. However, the Adivasi rebels later entered into a truce with the authorities.

I revisited the Joypur camp in April 2005. It looked the same. Robin Hembrom, the active student leader, was now a teacher. Satyanath Tudu was the new headmaster of the school. He was proud that one of his students, Bijoy Tudu, had passed his school finals from the nearby Bongaigaon High school with a first division. It has been a decade since these Santhal "refugees" began living at this camp. A decade is a long time. I was not surprised to learn that Birsa Kujur was no more. Nagen Ram Kahar, the camp president, told me the camp still housed 17,000 people. Fear and mistrust have kept them there. I met Lakshi and Jashmi Hembrom, two brave women widowed by the riots. I have detailed their stories in the chapters to follow.

How Marina Kropi Escaped Death

October 17, 2005. The place: a desolate road near the village of Charchim, in Southern Assam's Karbi Anglong district. Around 5.30 in the morning, Marina Kropi boarded a bus in the tiny, militant-infested village of Zirikindeng, and was on her way to Diphu, the district headquarters. Suddenly, after travelling for just about 12 kilometres, her bus came to a halt. If Marina is alive today, it's because of her split second decision. "I am a Garo," she told the armed men in black, clutching two little girls, Hom Sira and Hunali Tisopi, close to her chest. As the militants waylaid the bus and began dragging her fellow passengers out, Marina, 35, had already taken off her pekok, a traditional scarf worn by women of the Karbi tribe. This saved her. She was not in the group of Karbi tribespeople whom the killers lined up on the road, hands tied behind their backs.

Soon Marina and the two little Karbi girls she was holding would witness the most barbaric scene, humans being hacked to death with machetes, a scene that would haunt them all their lives. In that single massacre, twenty two passengers, all Karbis, were slaughtered by Dimasa rebels. They then walked away to raid Charchim, a Karbi village, burning homes and killing fifteen more. Six more Karbis were found dead a day later at the nearby village of Prseck.

On September 26, 2005, three Dimasa auto-rickshaw drivers had been found dead by the roadside near the town of Manza. This had at first seemed like an isolated incident. But it soon turned into full-scale violence between the two tribes that, along with a sprinkling of other ethnic communities such as Garos, Kukis and Bodos, inhabit the district of Karbi Anglong (area: 10,500 square kilometres). In the three-week-long orgy of violence that followed, 88 people were officially confirmed killed, 76 of whom were Karbis. 44,747 people from around 200 affected villages were put up at 55 relief camps in the district. Significantly, more than 37,000 people at these relief camps were Karbis, clearly indicating that people from this tribe have faced the brunt of the attacks despite being the majority ethnic group in the district. Karbi leaders concluded that there was a definite pattern in the killings and thought the Dimasa rebels had planned it well.

"We won't call it an ethnic battle as there has been hardly any retaliation by the Karbis," Tung-e Nongloda, publicity secretary of the United People's Democratic Solidarity (UPDS), a Karbi militant group, told me later. He said Dimasa villagers were evacuated from vulnerable villages before the rebel Dima Halam Daoga (DHD) launched its "organized killings." DHD chief Dilip Nunisa, who had shared a room with Nongloda during his college days, denied the charge. "My boys were not behind the massacre of Karbis. It could be plain retaliation by Dimasa villagers or the Black Widow group trying to avenge the killing of the three Dimasa auto-rickshaw drivers," Nunisa told me from his base in North Cachar Hills, a Dimasa-majority district that adjoins Karbi Anglong. The police did not find any evidence of the involvement of the ragtag and bobtail Black Widow group, a breakaway DHD faction headed by one of the DHD founders, Jewel Garlossa.

Denials notwithstanding, the authorities blamed the DHD and the UPDS of having "violated ceasefire ground rules," thereby indicating their involvement in the violence. The UPDS, fighting for "self-rule" for the Karbis, had entered into a ceasefire agreement with the Government on May 23, 2002, while the DHD, promising the Dimasas a separate Dimaraji state, had signed a truce with the authorities on January 1, 2003. That the two militant groups were active players during the mayhem, despite being in ceasefire mode, was proved on October 19, 2005 when nine UPDS cadres – four old members and five newly inducted ones – were killed by DHD rebels at Tamulbari, a village near the town of Diphu. UPDS leaders later said that upon learning that some DHD militants were camping at a nearby village, planning attacks on Karbis, their cadres had rushed there only to be ambushed by waiting DHD rebels.

Is there something more to the current bloodshed in Karbi Anglong? Many Karbi leaders felt the DHD was engaged in what they call an "expansionist campaign." They said that as the DHD was fighting for a Dimaraji state comprising the whole district of North Cachar Hills as well as parts of Karbi Anglong and Nagaon districts, it was likely that the rebel group was bent on pushing the Karbis out from Dhunsiri and other areas in Karbi Anglong where Dimasas were a majority. Issues as intricate and highly localised as these have time and again put Assam on the boil, leading to ethnic strife and insurgency. Often, militant groups seeking to represent different ethnic groups either start these confrontations on their own as part of their own turf wars or side with their respective communities to push their agenda, making things murkier.

Chapter I

THE BLACK 1996 MORNING THAT CHANGED TILLOTTAMA'S LIFE

November 19, 1996. There was a nip in the early morning air as is usual in Assam during this time of the year. Romel Chandra Basumatary, a 52-year-old primary schoolteacher had a quick breakfast and left his tin-roofed home in Banargaon, located in Western Assam's Kokrajhar district, for the village market nearby.

Tillottama Basumatary

It was around eight in the morning, and the bazaar was coming to life. Kameshwar Daimary, a farmer, parked his bicycle in front of a pan shop to buy a packet of bidis. "A truck pulled up right near my bicycle and the men who were in it started firing madly at everyone around. Then they got down from the vehicle and started firing again. I fled to the river bank nearby and watched the mayhem," Kameshwar, 46, told this writer at Banargaon, 260 kilometres west of Guwahati, in early April 2005.

Romel fell to the ground, never to rise again. So did Santa Ram Brahma, 18, Swgwmdao Brahma, 21, Sunil Basumatary, 25, and Thojendra Basumatary, 40. Two women, Purnima Basumatary and Nila Basumatary, succumbed to their injuries at a hospital in the district town of Kokrajhar, nine kilometres away.

Today, a shed for people to sit inside while waiting for buses has been built at the spot where this incident occurred, in memory of these "martyrs." The shed bears mute testimony to the fifteen-minute blitzkrieg by the rebels that changed the lives of many in this sprawling village of around 40,000 people. It is believed that those gunmen belonged to the outlawed National Democratic Front of Boroland (NDFB), an organization formed on October 3, 1986 with a pledge to fight for an independent Bodo homeland.

We walked past the Banargaon High School on a newly built pebbled road to Romel's home, a compound with three houses, surrounded by a bamboo fence. A framed photograph of the deceased had been put up at the entrance to what looked like the main house. A mud-plastered thatch-roofed structure on bamboo stilts right at the entrance to the compound was, of course, the granary.

Wearing a pale-yellow dokhona – the traditional wrap-around dress of Bodo women – and a white blouse, Romel's wife Tillottama, 56, organized chairs for us in her courtyard. A mother of four, two sons and two daughters, she was quite forthcoming in her replies to my questions about the tragedy in her life, her struggle since the death of her husband and the challenges that she faced.

"I was dazed when I saw my husband dead, lying in a pool of blood. I knew my life was shattered, but right then I also realized that I had to live for the sake of my children," Tillottama said, tears rolling down her cheeks despite her efforts at putting up a brave front. Her life as the head of the family had begun at that moment.

Resting her chin on her palms, Tillottama recalled the first few days of her life without her husband, who as head of the family, used to take care of all matters concerning finances, organizing the provisions etc. "Whatever money we had was spent on performing the last rites and so on. For a few days, my mind was a blank. I did not know what to do."

Within days, Tillottama began doing the rounds of the Deputy Commissioner's office in Kokrajhar to obtain the ex-gratia amount of Rs. 100,000 that the State Government used to pay then to the next of kin of people killed in militant violence. (The amount has since been raised to Rs. 3 lakh). Simultaneously, she began visiting the offices of the Deputy Inspector of Schools, also in Kokrajhar, to complete the formalities so that she could receive the family pension.

"I had to make around forty visits to the DC's office for two years after my husband's death before I received Rs. 70,000 as ex-gratia," Tillottama said. Neither she, nor villagers such as Kameshwar seemed to know why the authorities did not pay them the entire ex-gratia amount of Rs. 100,000. District officials in Kokrajhar could not say why only Rs. 70,000 was paid as ex-gratia to Tillottama. "Perhaps during that time it was paid in instalments," one of them said. If it took two years for Tillottama to get the ex-gratia amount, it was after four long years that she started receiving her family pension.

Life in the Bodo dominated western and northern Assam areas, the scene of both militant and ethnic upsurges in the nineties was such that killings had become almost routine, and, as such, the authorities and the society had gradually become less concerned about the impact of such violence on the affected families. A certain detachment seemed to have overtaken them. The manner in which the officials at the Kokrajhar DC and the DIS offices made Tillottama run around to get her dues, without any consideration for the fact that she had just lost her family's sole breadwinner clearly points to that conclusion.

So how did Tillottama manage her home before she got

some money? "I leased out the twelve bighas (nearly four acres) of land that we have to people from the village for cultivating paddy, on the condition that they would give me half the crop. I soon realized that the rice from our fields would last us just six months in a year," she said.

Tillottama realized that her elder son Milon, now 28, would have to get a job and start earning. Mother and son began job hunting seriously. In 1999, Milon was appointed a primary school teacher at the Ghoskata Lower Primary School nearby. But life in their household did not change much as Milon's was not a regular job. He was getting paid just Rs. 1,800 a month.

"For some reason, the local Deputy Inspector of Schools did not list Milon as the son of a victim of militant violence. That has deprived him of a regularized post which would have fetched him a salary of around Rs. 4,500 a month," Tillottama lamented.

This resolute woman poured her heart out to us, saying how, a year after her husband's untimely death at the hands of a bunch of trigger-happy militants, the Assam Plains Tribal Development Corporation turned down her plea for a small personal loan. "I approached the Corporation for a loan of Rs. 10,000 that I needed desperately for an eye operation. It rejected my request on the plea that they have no such provision," she added.

The Corporation bosses were right when they rejected Tillottama's petition for a personal loan as there was no provision to cater to the personal economic needs of the people. But where do ordinary villagers, hundreds of whom are survivors of violence across Assam, go in search of help, once they lose their key earning members? There is no official mechanism in place in the state to look after such people although Assam has been in the grip of militant and ethnic violence since the late eighties.

Tillottama's young daughter-in-law, Milon's wife, served us steaming hot tea. A crowd had gathered around us by then. Among them was Parbati, 35, wife of Thojendra Basumatary, one of those killed in the Banargaon massacre. Parbati has five children, two sons and three daughters. Her elder daughter is married, while the rest are in school.

"My husband was a muster-roll (semi-permanent) worker with the local Public Works Department. We had no land of our own and you can imagine my plight after he was killed. I had to feed my five children," Parbati said. For quite sometime, she survived on loans from villagers, and by doing odd jobs.

Like Tillottama, Parbati too received only Rs. 70,000, and not a lakh as ex-gratia payment from the authorities. And she too doesn't know why. But this frail woman made good use of her money, buying six bighas (1 bigha = 0.33 acre) of land and leasing it out for half the crop in return. "I get rice enough to feed my family for four months a year," she said with a vacant look on her face.

For almost everything needed to run her home, Parbati

has to depend on the Rs. 1,800 that she earns every month by working as a casual helper at the PWD office in Kokrajhar. "I hope my job gets regularized. I will then be assured of a monthly salary that I cannot do without," she said, and excused herself.

It was already late in the evening and Parbati had to cook for the children at home. On all working days, she would have to catch the 8 a.m. bus to Kokrajhar to reach the office on time. She would return home after dusk and then begin her routine chores of cooking and looking after the children.

The sun had turned a bright orange. I took leave of Tillottama and decided to see the structure that was built in memory of those who had died that November morning. The pinkish-brown marble memorial, listing the names of those killed that day, stood tall amid the vast paddy fields by the roadside. Many such cenotaphs dot the towns and countryside in the Bodo heartland, indicating just how much violence has rocked the area.

This neat memorial in Banargaon was erected by the All Bodo Students' Union. The influential student group's emblem of crossed swords and a shield was prominently positioned at the top. Three young Bodo girls, wearing bright yellow dokhonas, walked past.

They were certainly aware that the NDFB was at that point in truce mode and was ready to talk peace with New Delhi. The rebel group signed a formal ceasefire agreement with the Government on May 25, 2005. One of the girls looked back. She seemed to think everything would soon be all right - the NDFB would perhaps bid adieu to arms and its cadres emerge from hiding. If only those gunmen had not killed those simple, innocent folks at Banargaon that day. But such is insurgent politics — kill innocent people, target symbols of governmental authority, catch the attention of the government, and then bargain.

Chapter II

SURVIVORS OF TERROR: PARIAHS IN SOCIETY?

Anita Mashahary and Janaki Brahma have many things in common. Both are young Bodo women who were married to the then top leaders of the powerful All Bodo Students' Union. Both of them have been widowed in their prime.

That is not all. As though it was not enough that their husbands had been silenced by

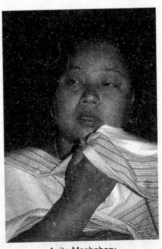

Anita Mashahary

the cruel "dance of death" of militants or some unknown armed rivals, they were also shunned by the society in which they lived, at least during the early days following their personal tragedies. People avoided them mostly because they were afraid of incurring the wrath of those who had killed their husbands.

Anita's and Janaki's stories have given the lie to the general belief that society cushions and protects the survivors of terror, especially if they are women who have lost their husbands or sons to violence. As a result, most of these women have had to strengthen their resolve to meet the challenges of life and move on, independently.

Anita, 32, lives with her 13-year-old son Jwrang and 10-year-old daughter Hatarkhi at Daularpara, a roadside village 45 kilometres north-west of Kokrajhar, in western Assam. The courtyard of her tin-roof home is neat. Clad in a traditional green dokhona, she was tending her lovely pink bougainvillaea when I visited her in early April, 2005.

She welcomed us warmly into her small living room. There was a framed photograph of her husband Bagrangsu Mashahary next to the TV. Another hung from a wall. Bagrangsu had been in student politics for a long time, and had held senior positions with the ABSU from 1987 until 1995, first as a leader of the Ramfalbil unit of the student organization, and then as a member of its Central Committee.

He married Anita, a schoolteacher, in February 1991. Life was quite smooth for the Mashaharys. In 1996, a new political party emerged in the Bodo heartland. It was called the People's Democratic Front (PDF) and was supposed to be close to the National Democratic Front of Boroland (NDFB), a militant group fighting to achieve an independent Bodo homeland.

"I didn't want him to join the PDF. But he was forced to join the new party by its founders and others even before his term in the ABSU had ended," Anita said. She perhaps had a premonition of impending danger after her husband was appointed secretary of the PDF's Kokrajhar district unit. After all, Bodo politics of the time – both mainstream as well as insurgent politics – was murky, to say the least.

The ABSU and all groups aligned to it were virtually at "war" with the NDFB, and the PDF, therefore, was seen by these forces as a group out to neutralize them. The emergence on the scene around the same time (1996) of the Bodo Liberation Tigers (BLT), a new rebel group, which sought to achieve the same goal (of a separate Bodo state within India) as that of ABSU and its allies, made the area a battle zone.

Now there were two heavily-armed insurgent groups seeking to represent the Bodos: the BLT and the NDFB. This obviously led to a turf war as both the playing field and political space available was quite small. This resulted in a bitter fratricidal feud in the area, and people like Anita's and Janaki's husbands had to pay the price for being involved in the messy politics of the time.

The BLT went on to sign a peace agreement with the Government on February 10, 2003. This brought the curtains down on its insurrection. A total of 2,641 BLT rebels laid down arms on December 26, 2003. The agreement led to the BLT giving up its demand for a separate Bodo state within the country. Instead, a 40-member elective politico-administrative structure with maximum autonomy, called the Bodoland Territorial Council (BTC), was created. But for the two women, sadly, peace came too late.

Anita lost her composure and sobbed as she related the events of that fateful day, October 13, 2000, when Bagrangsu was kidnapped and killed. "It was around 2.30 in the afternoon. Three cars drove up to our home. Some armed men got down and rushed inside. They took away my husband and another youth," she said. Bagrangsu's body, with bullet wounds and with his hands tied behind his back, was found on the banks of the river Swrmanga three days later. The other youth was released the very next day.

Bagrangsu may have been caught in the cross-currents of the local politics of the time, but the way society responded, practically shunning Anita and her two little children in the aftermath of his death, was surprising. "For a long time after my husband's death, hardly anybody visited us, perhaps out of fear of being linked to the PDF. Some people may have sympathized with us, but they kept away. Perhaps they thought that they would be targeted by those who killed my husband," Anita said.

Till today, Anita has not come to terms with the fact that her husband was killed by people belonging to her own community (Bodos) and that the society in which she lived did nothing to put her life back on track after the tragedy. "I expected those around us to treat me and my children sympathetically. After all, neither I, nor my children were involved in politics in any way," Anita lamented. The ABSU, of course, helped her perform her husband's shradh ceremony, but that was under the organization's banner. No individual ABSU member came forward to render any assistance thereafter.

Two years later, and after 30 or more visits to the Kokrajhar Deputy Commissioner's office, Anita received Rs. 100,000 that was due to her from the government as ex-gratia payment. "I have no fixed income now, and depend on half the paddy that is given to me by those who till my field. I need a job badly," she said. Anita is studying for her B.A degree at the Janata College nearby and wants to give her children the best she can. "Melodious music is the medicine of my life," she said, pointing at her collection of audio cassettes.

Like Anita's, Janaki's husband Rupswrang Brahma, too, was a senior ABSU leader (he was Speaker of the ABSU's Kokrajhar district unit) before he was inducted into the PDF. One day, in 2001, someone reached him at his native Sialmari village (No 2) in Kokrajhar district, and said he was wanted in the nearby sub-divisional town of Gossaigaon in connection with some work relating to his NGO, Sikhnajhar Forest & Land Protection

Committee. Rupswrang was last seen by some villagers having tea at a roadside tea stall at Kachugaon, a small town.

"After a week, we somehow received information that my husband had been killed. We haven't found the body yet," thirty year old Janaki said at her home in Serfanguri, a highway-side town, tears rolling down her eyes. Her daughter Miranda, now four, was just about ten months old when her father disappeared all of a sudden.

Janaki Brahma

It was not Janaki, a virtually uneducated mother of an infant (she studied up to Class IV), who was expected to go to the local police station and lodge a missing person report following the disappearance of her husband. But her relatives or the village elders were certainly expected to lodge an FIR with the police. "But the situation was such at that time that no one could summon enough courage to lodge a missing report with the police. It was only after a month that an FIR was filed at the Serfanguri Police Station," Janaki said.

Clutching Miranda to herself, Janaki recalled that neither the police nor the organizations which her husband had served for so long took any serious initiative to search for his body. "I did not receive help from the people around me on any front. I never even got any ex-gratia payment as I did not know how to go about claiming it," Janaki said, sitting near a reeling wheel in her courtyard.

Significantly, neither Anita nor Janaki want to mobilize women survivors like them, and form a group to look after themselves and face life together. "I have lost faith in organizations and groups. I don't even want to take up any such initiative at an individual level," Janaki said. It is clear that people like them have lost faith in civil society for its indifferent attitude to their misfortune and for not contributing anything to help them deal with their trauma.

Today, she depends solely on the rice she gets from those who cultivate her two-acre field. "Half of the produce goes to the growers. Still, I sometimes have enough rice to last us a year," Janaki said. She weaves clothes on the hand loom that is dear to her and sells them to retailers in the local market for some extra income.

The only people who backed her throughout her ordeal were her parents. "They still help me in whatever small ways they can. They work as my emotional support system," Janaki said. She has forgiven all her village-folk for abandoning her when she needed them the most. "I'm happy they come to visit me these days. Now my only dream and challenge is to see Miranda do well in life. I need help for my child's upbringing, but don't know where it will come from," Janaki said, before bidding us goodbye.

Chapter III

HOW LAKSHI HEMBROM LOST HER POWER TO THINK

Clutching a pile of books in one hand and a tattered jute sack in the other, Shome Hasda and Barka Mardi look intently at the cars that whiz past. Classes over, the two four-year-olds leave their rickety primary school that has no benches or walls and walk up to the highway (National Highway 31-C), which links Assam with the rest of India.

Lakshi Hembrom

The little ones with unkempt hair, clad in worn-out shorts and shirts that badly need a wash, idle around till dusk. For them, there is neither enough food, nor any comfort to lure them back home after school. Their huts, with roofs that are thatched or covered with plastic sheeting, are dingy and dark. Their parents hardly have any belongings. For Shome and Barka, the jute sacks are prized possessions, for they lay them on the mud floor at school to sit on during classes.

All the 17,000 odd Adivasi Santhal people live in such conditions at the Joypur relief camp, in Western Assam's Kokrajhar district, without proper sanitation, educational facilities or healthcare. For almost a decade, they have been living in this manner in nearly 2900 such hutments on this highway-side settlement that passes off as a relief camp. Ever since the Bodo-Santhal riots that rocked the district of Kokrajhar in 1996, and once again in 1998, these people are waging a grim battle for survival.

The official count put the death toll during the orgy of violence in the district at 468. Besides, more than 300,000 people, belonging to both communities, were uprooted from their homes. Till mid-2005, 32 such relief camps still functioned in Kokrajhar district alone, housing 101,907 people, including 26,811 women and 36,126 children. Lakshi Hembrom, 45, is one of them. A survivor, she has seen a violent past, is going through a miserable present and is headed towards an uncertain future.

Nagen Ram Kahar, a portly man in his fifties who is the president of the Joypur camp, sends for Lakshi as I turn up at the settlement on a warm afternoon in early April, 2005. Soon, a frail woman clad in a checked lungi and a green cotton scarf arrives and settles down for a conversation, surrounded by a group of fellow refugees.

On May 17, 1996, this Adivasi Santhal woman's husband, Betka Tudu, was killed by a rampaging mob. Often, Lakshi would recall that horrific night when all hell broke loose. A mob descended in the area where she had a hutment and started attacking the Adivasis. As the Adivasis ran for safety, they realized the rampaging raiders were torching their homes. Betka Tudu was not as lucky. He fell to a blow from a sharp machete.

The Bodos and the Adivasi Santhals have lived in the area for years, but they never killed each other before. Tudu's death and the prevailing situation at that time immediately left Lakshi and her four children homeless, hungry and traumatized. Lakshi had no time to even mourn her husband's death. After the last rites, following a post-mortem, she led her three children to the relative safety of the Joypur camp.

"Life has been tough ever since that mayhem to which I lost my husband. The meagre ration that the authorities supply us is just not enough," Lakshi says. The refugees in the camp have usually been getting government rations for only 10 days a month – 620 and 400 grams of rice for each adult and child respectively per day. In the initial years, refugees in the camp used to be provided about 50 grams of salt a day. But that has stopped coming now.

So how does she manage to feed herself and her children? "Often, we survive on one meal a day. I also join my fellow refugees in hunting for wild roots and tubers. Of course, we look for rats, too, all over the place. Rats can be delicious," Lakshi says. Satyanath Tudu, the young Headmaster of the middle school at the camp, senses my uneasiness. "Our people eat rats. It is a sort of tradition," he explains.

Lakshi may have been broken by her husband's brutal death. But her toddler son's death in 1998 has left her shattered. "I lost my child simply because I could not pay for his treatment. I'm sure if I had had even a little money, I could have saved him. I see his face before my eyes all the time," she weeps.

Lakshi doesn't know if she will ever leave the camp and settle down elsewhere. She had arrived here from the shack that she and her family had stayed in for years at the nearby settlement of Radhanagar Sonapur. I am not calling it a village because it never was one. The place was a part of the Chirang Reserve Forest, and as such a protected area. But as in many such reserved forests across Assam, encroachers cleared the trees and settled down illegally. The Adivasis who settled at that place named it Radhanagar Sonapur.

There is a relative calm in the area now. But Lakshi cannot return to Radhanagar Sonapur. That settlement has since been occupied by Bodo settlers. They, too, are encroachers. So, Lakshi is actually a homeless person who is heading a family without a home. She has hardly any income of her own, and her twenty two-year-old son is a daily wage earner who cannot meet the expenses of the family of four. Lakshi has already spent the Rs. 95,000 she got from the authorities as ex-gratia payment after her husband's death. She does not remember whether or not she had received the remaining Rs. 5,000.

Kahar, the camp president, likes to intervene and make his point. He says that they would all like to leave the camp and settle down elsewhere provided the government gives them land and money to build houses. I ask Lakshi for her personal opinion. "I'm helpless. I have lost the power to think. I shall agree to whatever our leaders decide," she says, her sullen face expressionless. She starts muttering, "There's no point lamenting my husband's death or my fate. I know I have to fight for the rest of my life to survive."

Just then, Jashmi Hembrom, 42, another survivor walks in to join her. Her husband, Lakhan Murmu, was killed on August 30, 1998 near the place where they lived in Gaurinagar, close to the Joypur camp, during yet another bout of bloody violence between the Bodos and the Adivasis. Like Lakshi, Jashmi and her husband were encroachers who had set up home in Gaurinagar.

A distraught Jashmi, along with her teenage daughter, sought refuge at the house of a member of her community. "I realized my future was bleak, so when I got a match for my daughter, I married her off without much thought," she says. Jashmi's daughter moved out with her husband, a farmer. Month after month, Jashmi lived alone, wondering all the time how she could take control of her life.

Unlike Lakshi, Jashmi appeared to have much more will power. She managed to collect the ex-gratia amount of Rs. 100,000 from the district authorities, gave a portion of the money to her daughter, deposited the rest in a bank, purchased some cattle and was managing to earn just enough to take care of herself. Still, life for her was tough. And so she did not refuse when a man she knew offered to marry her. Jashmi remarried a year ago.

"Life has hardly changed for me. I have been living in this camp for nearly a decade now with nowhere to go," she says. Others living in the camp, such as Robin Hembrom, 29, a teacher, join Kahar in demanding land for the people living in camps like the one in Joypur. "We have been pleading with the Forest Department to de-reserve the settlements where we lived before the riots brought us to the camps. The authorities can then give us the land documents," Robin says.

Land or no land, life has to go on. But the sad thing is that there are hardly any NGOs working in the area to reduce the misery of these people. Besides the primary school, the camp also has a middle school, Joypur Manglajhara ME School. Set up in 1996, the school has six teachers who depend on donations for their meagre salaries. The Lutheran

World Service (LWS) provides the salary of one of the teachers. In fact, the Christian missionaries belonging to the LWS are about the only people from any non-government organization working among these displaced people, although in a very small way.

In the middle of 2005, some Adivasi groups had pressed for a speedy rehabilitation of people like Lakshi, Jashmi and hundreds of people belonging to the community who are living in the camp. They had even threatened to boycott or oppose the maiden elections to the Bodoland Territorial Council (BTC) if the issue was not resolved by then. Later, however, the groups announced their decision to participate in the polls (the BTC polls took place in May 2005) taking into account political exigencies. The BTC − the politico-administrative structure that people in the Bodo heartland got in 2003 after a protracted agitation for a "homeland" − might eventually come to the aid of the riot-hit people on its own. Even then, the void in Lakshi's life cannot be filled. She will continue to exist, not live. But that, perhaps, is her destiny.

Chapter IV

LIFE'S CRUEL JOKE ON KAMRUN NISSA

Kamrun Nissa was just into her teens when she got married in 1976. Her husband Faiz Ahmed, a contractor, was associated with the Congress party. He had a modest home right in the middle of Tengakhat, a nondescript town with potholed roads on the way to Duliajan, headquarters

Kamrun Nissa

of Oil India Limited (OIL), in eastern Assam's Dibrugarh district.

Life was just fine for Kamrun Nissa. Her husband was working hard, trying to bag as much work as he could, besides doing everything possible to climb the Congress party ladder. Faiz's determination paid off. He went on to become the local Block Congress president. Faiz had no reason to complain about his home front either, for he had a devoted wife.

A year passed by, and then another. Kamrun Nissa was getting restive by the day. No doubt her husband's elder brother Kamrud's family was there for company. But that did not ease her restlessness. After all she had failed to bear Faiz a child so far. This thought troubled Kamrun Nissa no end. She was a lady with a heart of gold. Soon, she made up her mind and prevailed upon her husband to take a second wife.

It was the early eighties. Assam was in the grip of a massive anti-foreigner uprising. The All Assam Students' Union (AASU) was spearheading one of independent India's biggest mass movements. Its leaders had taken a vow to oust the illegal Bangladeshi migrants, who, they feared, could outnumber the indigenous people of Assam. A section of those active in this stir wanted more aggressive action.

The culture of violence was growing roots in the state. The United Liberation Front of Asom (ULFA) was in place, after that meeting at the Rang Ghar in Sivasagar on April 7, 1979. These fledgling rebels who met at this famous amphitheatre of the Ahom royalty sowed their dream of a "sovereign, socialist

Assam." Killings, threats and intimidations were slowly emerging in the state.

Faiz was gradually consolidating his position in the local Congress politics. He was pleased, and more good news was coming his way. "I was so happy the day my husband got a baby boy through his second wife. I realized I had taken the right decision in getting him to marry again," Kamrun Nissa tells me at her home one afternoon in late April, 2005, her voice almost drowned out by the sound of the pre-monsoon rains hitting the tin roof above. Soon, Faiz had a second son.

It was 1991. The Assam Assembly elections were approaching. There was talk in Congress circles that Faiz was to be given the party ticket to contest the Duliajan seat. The party was on a comeback trail as the Asom Gana Parishad (AGP) government headed by Chief Minister Prafulla Kumar Mahanta had been dismissed a couple of months ago, in November 1990, and President's rule had been imposed. The reason for this was that ULFA's activities had peaked, and New Delhi had concluded that law and order had collapsed in the state during the tenure of this regional political party.

January 20, 1991 began on an uneventful note for Faiz. After a late afternoon cup of tea, he was playing with his sons, Farid, 7, and Zakir, 5, flying paper planes in front of his home. It was around 4.30 in the afternoon. The market at Tengakhat was coming to life with shoppers. Suddenly, a man approached him and asked if he was Faiz Ahmed. Within minutes, Faiz lay dead, shot by masked gunmen draped in shawls.

"I was inside, at home. I first thought it was the burst of firecrackers. When I rushed out, I realized to my horror that it was my husband who had been killed," Kamrun Nissa said. Faiz received four bullets in his chest and one in the shoulder. Little Farid watched his father crash onto the ground. Zakir was, of course, too young to fathom the enormity of the tragedy. The killers fled in a getaway car, dropping a shawl as they left.

The next day (January 21, 1991), Assam Congress veteran and former Chief Minister Hiteswar Saikia, accompanied by other senior party leaders, came to visit Faiz's family. He handed over an amount of Rs. 10,000 as an immediate relief in his individual capacity. Within three months, Saikia became the Chief Minister, having led the Congress to victory at the polls held in April.

He had not forgotten Faiz. Saikia directed his aides to get Faiz's wife a suitable government job as soon as possible. After all, his contribution to the party had been immense. But the Chief Minister's aides were soon to discover that the matter was not that simple, for Faiz had left behind two wives. Once again Kamrun Nissa made things easy. "I had already decided that if a job were to come our way, it was to go to her (the second wife). So when it did come in 1992, I told the authorities to give it to my late husband's second wife as she had two children to look after," she said.

The job at the local Sub-Deputy Collector's office at Tengakhat fetched the lady Rs. 1,800 a month. That eased the cash crunch a bit for the four-member family (two wives and the two children). For over a year, they had been looked after by Kamrun. The government released an ex-gratia amount of Rs. 100,000 to the bereaved family, two years after Faiz's death. This amount was shared equally between the wives. Two years passed by, with the two women struggling to make ends meet and bring up Farid and Zakir.

One day in 1994, the other woman disappeared, leaving her sons behind. "We searched for her all over the place, but couldn't trace her. Later, we came to know that she had re-married and left with her new husband," Kamrun Nissa recalled. No one came to collect or enquire about Farid and Zakir. "We realized that the two boys had been abandoned," she added.

But Kamrun Nissa was no ordinary woman. She took upon herself the responsibility of looking after the two boys. "After all, they are my husband's children. I cannot abandon them like their mother did," Kamrun Nissa said. Life had suddenly become much harder for her. "First, the source of funds dried up after she (the second wife) disappeared. Then, I had to take special care of the elder son Zakir who was still suffering from the trauma of having witnessed the fatal attack on his father," she said.

Zakir, who at the time of the tragedy was a Class IV student, was probably hit by post-traumatic stress disorder.

He used to keep repeating the number of the car apparently used by his father's killers, and would often say, "That's the car they used."

"For a year, Zakir did not sleep at night. He refused to go to school and I had to keep him on my lap most of the time. He was gripped by fear. It was tough bringing him back to a semblance of normalcy," Kamrun Nissa stated. But, with as caring a person as Kamrun Nissa around, whom the boys love and regard as their own mother, things were kept under control despite heavy odds.

The police took up the case and rounded up several shopkeepers from near Faiz's home. But till today, Kamrun Nissa is not aware either of the identities of those who had taken her husband's life, or why they did. "He (her husband) had no enmity with anyone. Besides, we never received any intimation or warning from any quarter whatsoever," she said. No group or individual had claimed responsibility for killing Faiz, and the police, too, could not arrive at any conclusion. In such cases, they usually do not.

Kamrun Nissa was finding it difficult to make ends meet. She decided to approach the Deputy Commissioner in Dibrugarh. "I mainly asked that the job that my husband's second wife had left behind be given to me. The DC asked me to obtain a written note from her saying she was quitting her job and that she had no problem if it was now given to me. But how could I have located her; she had disappeared,"

Kamrun Nissa said, expressing surprise at the district magistrate's attitude.

"Neither the party to which my husband belonged (Congress), nor the society as came forward to help me in my hour of crisis. Whatever help I got was at the individual level," she lamented. Kamrun Nissa then decided to knock at the doors of the Lok Adalat, a fast-track court of justice, which holds monthly sittings at the district town of Dibrugarh.

"For a couple of years starting in 1996, I used to visit Dibrugarh every month to appear at the Lok Adalat to seek justice. I primarily wanted the job that disappeared with the sudden exit of the other woman (Faiz's second wife)," she said. But justice never came, and Kamrun Nissa, unable to afford the fifty to hundred rupees that was needed for each trip to and from Dibrugarh, finally gave up hope on the Lok Adalat.

By now, she knew she could no longer depend on the government or the judiciary for justice, and resolved to face life on her own. She consolidated all her available resources and somehow managed to build three sheds in front of her house. Today, she earns Rs. 1,600 a month as rent from the three shops that have come up in those sheds. The boys were growing up and Kamrun Nissa obviously was in need of more money.

In 2002, she managed to get a job as a helper at the local Anganwadi centre. This brings her a meagre Rs. 500 a month. Every morning, she walks the half kilometre distance to the centre to arrive at the place by 7 a.m. At the end of her two-hour stint of duty, she walks back home, and starts the domestic chores of the day, doing household work, cooking for the boys, taking care of the younger one's studies and making sure that Farid learns how to run a shop properly.

Zakir, her younger boy, had some good news coming his way. He was among the few hundred children across Assam to be chosen for the Rs. 600-a-month stipend by Project Aashwas to pursue his studies. This assistance was provided by the National Foundation for Communal Harmony, New Delhi. This Assam Police-UNICEF venture is aimed at assisting child victims of insurgency and ethnic violence in the state.

Zakir has since appeared in his school final examinations and is looking forward to continuing his studies. And Kamrun Nissa is bent on ensuring that he can fulfil his dream of earning a degree. She keeps up a cheerful front to make sure the boys stay happy.

Kamrun Nissa lost her husband to those hooded gunmen's bullets, but she was destined to be a mother. She became one, a caring mother to two boys who would otherwise have been virtually orphaned.

Kamrun Nissa symbolizes the spirit of womanhood, and lives on to tell her story.

Chapter V

FAMILY TIES COST BHARATI DEAR

The seventies were a mix of the sweet and the sour for the Gandhians, Uma Rajkonwar and his wife Damayanti, residents of Ujjani Konwar, near the village of Lakuwa in eastern Assam's Sivasagar district. The Rajkonwars, who led a quiet life, decided to get their son, Dimba, an employee of the Assam State Transport

Bharati Rajkonwari

Corporation, married. Everyone in the family, particularly Dimba's eight siblings, was very happy.

When Nityananda Gogoi – an Indian Oil Corporation official working at the refinery hospital in Digboi – received the proposal from the Rajkonwars for his daughter Bharati's hand, he and his wife readily agreed for the Rajkonwars were a well-known family who had participated in the freedom struggle. Uma Rajkonwar had been honoured with the "tamrapatra" for his involvement in the freedom struggle, and the family was well liked.

It was 1971. Bharati, the eldest of the Gogois' seven children, got married to Dimba Rajkonwar. Soon, the couple left for Shillong, the then capital of undivided Assam, where Dimba was posted. A little more than a year later, he got a transfer to Dibrugarh, which was closer to both his own home and his wife's.

Dimba and his young wife Bharati set up home in Dibrugarh, the nerve-centre of the tea growing district, and were settling down. Bharati was by now working with the State Public Works Department. Both husband and wife had a normal work schedule. Dimba, an Ahom, whose ancestors had ruled Assam for 600 years from 1228 AD, was actively involved with the Chailung Sukapha Memorial Committee. Sukapha was the first King of the Ahom dynasty which had been victorious in warding off successive Mughal forays over the centuries into Assam.

The couple had their first child in 1975, a son. Bharati

became busier than before. Dimba did his bit to help her. He was filled with joy and resolved to bring up the child as best as he could. He continued to be actively involved in things dear to his heart. Aside from being associated with the Sukapha Memorial Committee, Dimba was an active member of the Asom Sahitya Sabha, Assam's apex socio-literary body. He used to write, but had not yet published his works, which were read perhaps by Bharati and just a few of his close friends.

It was 1979. The United Liberation Front of Asom was born. Dimba's brother Rajiv Rajkonwar, the sixth of Uma and Damayanti's nine children, was among the youth who had met at the Rang Ghar. The day was April 7, 1979. The rebel group was to change Assam's political and security situation.

Rajiv had already vowed during the Umpha Puja, an Ahom festival which comes once in 12 years, to bring back the glorious days of the Ahom era, the days when his ancestors had ruled Assam. That was after the police tortured him because of his role as a local leader of a youth outfit, the Asom Jatiyatabadi Yuba Chatra Parishad. Earlier, he had vowed to remain a vegetarian, but during that festival, he had consumed offerings from the Ahom temple at the village, a mixture of pork, beef and mutton and broken that promise.

Rajiv Rajkonwar had become a rebel. One day, he fell at his father's feet, made an offering of tamul-pan and told him that he was going away, to fight for the cause of an "independent" Assam. He would return either dead or with freedom for his state. Rajiv Rajkonwar went on to become Arabinda Rajkhowa, a dreaded guerrilla chieftain and chairman of the outlawed ULFA. That was the last time that the Rajkonwars saw Rajiv.

Life was to change for Dimba and Bharati. They, after all, were members of the ULFA chief's family. Bharati remembered that they were very harassed in those days. She recalled the roar of the Army trucks that would break the stillness of the night. The soldiers would jump out of their vehicles, surround their house, and barge in. "Usually, a junior officer would lead the troops. He would irritate us no end by asking us the same questions over and over again. They wanted information about Rajiv. The Army visited us five to six times, and at times troops, accompanied by policemen, used to arrive at our home at midnight," Bharati, now 57, told me at her modest home in a by-lane in Dibrugarh in early May, 2005. There was a time when the sight of the approaching Army troopers was enough to make the males of the families living in Ujjani Konwar flee to the nearby forests. The villagers had, in any case, already answered the Army's questions about Rajiv's whereabouts: they knew nothing about it.

Once, Dimba was picked up by security men and booked under the Terrorist and Disruptive Activities (Prevention) Act or TADA, a stringent anti-terror law. He was freed on bail about a month later. This perhaps was part of the tactics adopted by those in charge of counter insurgency in the state at that time, in order to put pressure upon the battle-hardened rebels who were keeping the men in uniform on their toes. Harassment of innocent family members, after all, can be a traumatic experience for the rebels who, too, are humans.

"We never used to talk about or discuss Rajiv (Arabinda Rajkhowa). My husband also never used to tell me anything about his elusive brother," Bharati said, sitting in her living room. She recalled that sleep was a problem, for the soldiers used to come calling frequently to look for any information on Arabinda.

The family started getting apprehensive after batches of ULFA rebels began surrendering to the authorities. Many of them were used by the police, Army and the paramilitary to spot ULFA militants or lead them to their hideouts or safe-houses. Some surrendered ULFA men, who came to be known as SULFA cadres, started indulging in excesses and became almost a law unto themselves. "I remember having an eerie feeling, as though something terrible was waiting to happen," Bharati said.

August 11, 1998. The sun had set, but it was still quite hot and humid. It was around 6.45. Dimba Rajkonwar was pacing up and down in the State Transport Corporation yard, in front of his office in the heart of Dibrugarh. As an officer of the Transport Corporation, his duty hours were not yet over for that day. The night buses were yet to leave for Guwahati and other cities and towns in the state. The place was not well lit, but still the visibility was not too bad.

Little did Dimba know that he was taking the last few breaths of his life. A motorbike rushed up from nowhere, and the riders pumped two bullets into Dimba from behind. He fell to the ground with a thud. His colleagues and bystanders rushed him to the Assam Medical College Hospital, not far away. But he was already dead, for the killers had attacked him at very close range. Dimba Rajkonwar died at the age of 54. The ULFA boss had lost a brother.

"I had just reached home from office. My sister rushed in and said baideu (sister) come with us, someone has shot at bhindeu (brother-in-law), he's in hospital," Bharati recalled that traumatic moment in her life. She made for her husband's office first and then the hospital. "But, he lay there, lifeless." The body was taken to Dimba's native Ujjani Konwar, where his father Uma and mother Damayanti were waiting to see their son, one last time. "Dimba has become a swahid (martyr)," Bharati quoted her father-in-law as having said at that time.

Dimba and Bharati's elder son was doing a course in computers in New Delhi when the tragedy occurred. Their younger son was a student of Class IX, while their daughter was in Class XII. "My life was suddenly shattered. I became a single parent, saddled with the responsibility of looking after my three young children," Bharati said. Significantly, the State Government, contrary to its normal practice, has not given her the mandatory ex-gratia payment of Rs. 100,000 till today.

"I remember requesting some ministers during the tenure of the Asom Gana Parishad Government (the party was in power in Assam at that time) and later approached Chief Minister Tarun Gogoi and other Congress leaders. But the ex-gratia payment never came," she lamented. Could it be that the authorities decided to deprive Bharati of her due ex-gratia payment just because she belongs to a family, one of whose members is a militant leader?

She, however, had some kind words for the Assam State Transport Corporation, her husband's employers. "The ASTC released most of my husband's deposits such as his Provident Fund and insurance dues. I am now waiting for his gratuity," Bharati said. She recalled with gratitude the sympathy of people around her after her husband's demise. "After all, my husband was a simple, innocent soul. People used to like him a lot," she said.

"My only resolve after the tragedy was to bring up my children well and make them independent in life," Bharati said. That she has done. Her daughter has completed her Masters in English literature, and is currently looking for a job. The elder son works in a private company and the younger son is doing a course in fashion design. "I had requested Chief Minister Gogoi for a job for my daughter. But there has been no response yet. I am still hoping the Government will do something for her," Bharati said.

This lady, unlike many survivors of violence like her across the state, is a woman with determination. She was shattered by the death of her husband, but has not given up on life. "I am really keen to form an organization to help those women widowed as a result of violence in Assam. Women like us need to take charge of our lives and move ahead despite the odds," Bharati said. Her husband's sisters at times tell her to join politics and try and become a people's representative.

What could Bharati possibly tell the ULFA chieftain Arabinda, her brother-in-law, should she come face to face with him? She said: "I shall tell him to stop violence and begin talks with the Government. I will tell him to restore peace in Assam by resolving their problems through a dialogue."

Bharati should be happy that the ULFA, in September 2005, nominated an 11-member People's Consultative Group, comprising individuals who do not belong to the organization, to talk peace with New Delhi. The Group held the first round of talks, attended by Prime Minister Manmohan Singh, in October 2005 to try and prepare the ground for direct negotiations between the ULFA and the Indian Government.

She has not received any special help from the Government for the untimely death of her husband at the hands of gunmen. Nor has she received any compensation. "But my only regret has been that the investigation into his death has not yielded any result so far," she said.

Dimba Rajkonwar's reply to Bharati's fears for his life was always the same. He would say that a person was destined to die at a certain time and place and nothing could change that. Bharati, however, doesn't seem to believe only in destiny. "He was killed just because he happened to be the brother of the ULFA Chairman," she said.

Looking straight at the framed portrait of her husband in the living room, Bharati said, "I cannot excuse or forgive my husband's killers. They snatched away my children's father." She managed a smile as she bid us goodbye.

I saw Bharati shutting the door behind us, not out of fear, but because the pre-monsoon rains came down heavy that night. The winds were strong too.

Chapter VI

HOW HEMOPROVA WAS DRIVEN TO THE BRINK

Summers can be quite sultry in Assam. Premadhar Konwar, 53, a generously proportioned man who worked at the Hindustan Fertiliser Corporation's plant at Namrup, in the eastern region of the state, returned to his company quarters from the market nearby. It was 8.40 in the evening. Handing

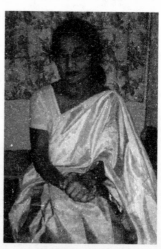

Hemoprova Konwar

over the purchases to his wife Hemoprova, Premadhar headed straight for a bath.

Having changed into a white dhoti and kurta, with a gamocha, the white-and-red Assamese hand-woven scarf, flung across his shoulder, Premadhar enquired if dinner was ready. The man followed a strict routine. The couple and their two sons had their dinner at 9.30 everyday. This night, too, the family had their dinner together. Premadhar shared the burden of the household work with his wife as much as he could. On this occasion too, he carried his used plate into the kitchen.

Hemoprova gave him tamul-pan. He put it quickly into his mouth. After sometime, Premadhar opened the front door of his house and went out into the small porch. It was rather dark, for the light at the Durgabari, a Durga temple in front of the Konwars' home, had not been switched on that night.

"I was inside, but saw him talking to someone. There were about four of them. Suddenly, I heard the sound of a gunshot. I remember screaming and rushing out. Then I fell unconscious," Hemoprova told me when I visited her at her home in Namrup, more than 500 kilometres from Guwahati, one damp May morning in 2005.

Premadhar fell down, dead. The killers had fired a single shot right at his head. June 27, 1993 was to change the lives of Hemoprova and her two sons, Preeti and Bibhuti Bhusan, forever. But who could have killed Premadhar, and why?

After all, he was just an ordinary employee in the Production Department of the HFC plant, not a high ranking executive. Premadhar was not involved in any politics whatsoever, not even of the local trade union variety.

The outlawed ULFA was still active, more so in and around Namrup and other parts of eastern Assam, despite the Army launching "Operation Bajrang" against the rebels in November 1990. At the time of Premadhar's death, the Army's second offensive against the ULFA, "Operation Rhino" – launched in September 1991 – was in full swing. At that time, the ULFA was not known to carry out random killings. But even then, could the outfit have been behind Premadhar's killing?

The bereaved family, following tradition, ate off plantain leaves for one whole month. The younger son Bibhuti, who was just eight, was happy eating that way, for he found it an interesting departure from the normal meals at the dining table. But Hemoprova, herself still in a daze after the tragedy, was worried on account of her elder son, Preeti. At that time around fourteen years old, Preeti was getting increasingly restive.

"He began to talk about taking revenge. He kept asking why his father was killed, why anyone would want to do that," Hemoprova said. Preeti Bhusan was probably suffering from post-traumatic stress disorder, and in the absence of any professional counselling, the family was unable to calm him down.

It is indeed strange that although Assam has been in the grip of insurgent violence and ethnic strife since the late eighties, the authorities have not thought it necessary to provide professional counselling to the survivors of violence. "I had to really work very hard in order to bring my son back to a semblance of normalcy," Hemoprova recalled.

She herself was fast sinking into a deep depression. "I stopped visiting anybody in case they thought that I had gone to them to seek help. I also hesitated to venture out into the market. I was apprehensive of the people's response. I was slowly becoming an emotional wreck," Hemoprova told me, sitting in the small living room of her house.

The lady was now required to head the household, but she was not in control of things around her. "I remember just sitting and doing nothing for long stretches of time. When my younger son would come to me for help with his school homework, I would send him away, asking him to manage on his own," Hemoprova said.

She became a recluse and started avoiding people, including her husband's colleagues. "One day, I was walking near my home when a company doctor stopped his car by my side and asked me why I was not talking to him. He wanted to know if I was avoiding him," Hemoprova recalled. The doctor gave her a few professional tips that could help her to regain some kind of normalcy with regard to her mental condition.

Her relatives, too, began to motivate her to face life and move ahead. Hemoprova did not visit her relatives for more than seven years after the incident. "It was only two years ago that I visited my father-in-law's home at Amguri (near Sivasagar) for the first time after I lost my husband. I had no option but to take charge of my life for the sake of my sons," she said.

Three years had passed and funds were fast depleting. True, her mother was giving her all possible help, including sending rice in bulk. But Hemoprova's need for a job became pressing. She approached Hiteswar Saikia, then Chief Minister of Assam, for a job, but did not get one. The State Government was most unhelpful. By now, there were scores of widows like Hemoprova across violence-wrecked Assam, and the authorities had perhaps become immune to human suffering.

Hemoprova was not given even the mandatory ex-gratia payment of Rs. 100,000 although her husband was felled by armed men. "Six months after the incident, I met the Deputy Commissioner at his office in Dibrugarh and handed him a petition detailing the circumstances under which my husband was killed. Till today, I haven't heard anything from the DC's office regarding the ex-gratia payment," she lamented.

The HFC, her husband's employers, had cleared the provident fund amount due to him. And Hemoprova was entitled to a monthly pension of Rs. 290 from the fertilizer company. But it was too meagre an amount. The HFC authorities had permitted Hemoprova and her two sons to continue staying at quarter No. 476 (Sector C), the house where the couple had started out their married life and raised their family. And where, on a dark night, the head of the family lost his life.

Leaders and members of the HFC plant's employees' union were working hard to get Hemoprova a job. Her husband after all had been liked by them all. Finally, the union leaders succeeded in their efforts. Hemoprova, now 45, was appointed on September 1, 1996 as a lower primary teacher in one of the schools run by the HFC plant at Namrup. She began with a salary of Rs. 3,500 per month.

The lady has really managed to return from the brink. "Once I got the job, I began with a clear focus: carry out my responsibility of teaching the school children to the best of my ability, and bring up my sons well," Hemoprova said. Premadhar had wanted his elder son to become a doctor or an Army officer. But life had charted out a different course for Preeti Bhusan. Today, this 26-year-old has a business enterprise of his own. "He is in a much better state of mind now, but if anything goes wrong, he still asks if it is because his father is not alive," Hemoprova said about Preeti Bhusan.

If Premadhar had wanted his elder son to join the Army or take up medicine, he had encouraged the younger son Bibhuti to take his dance lessons seriously. This was the course Bibhuti was to pursue in the years to come. After his high school finals, he joined a music college nearby. "Now, he can perform Sattriya, the traditional Assamese dance form introduced by the sixteenth century philosopher-saint Sri Sankardeva, Bihu and Bharatnatyam with ease," Hemoprova said.

If she is back on track today, it's entirely because of the support she got from her family, her husband's colleagues, particularly the trade union leaders at the HFC plant, her sense of responsibility towards her sons, and her goal of bringing them up well. The Government on its part has contributed nothing in bringing her shattered life back on track. "One can't expect much from any Government, but I expected the police to arrive at some conclusion about the identity of my husband's killers," Hemoprova said.

"Till my dying day, I would want to know why my husband was killed," she said, looking at his framed portrait hanging on the wall. Hemoprova looked solemn, but she still managed a smile. Her life revolves around her school, her family, and the temple which she visits every Monday. The centre of her life these days is her grandson Mrinmoy (Preeti Bhusan's son), whom she lovingly calls Pusku. Clutching the eight-month-old in her arms, Hemoprova bid us goodbye from the same porch where her husband was shot dead twelve years ago.

Life indeed has to go on.

Chapter VII

BHANUMATI AND RAKTIMA:
THEIR KIDS' MOM, DAD TOO

L ittle Phami has never seen her dad. This eight-year-old Class III student doesn't know what a dad is like. From the day she was born, her mother Bhanumati has been her father, too. All because two armed militants, posing as guests, descended on Bhanumati's home in the western Assam district town of Kokrajhar one morning and

Bhanumati

pumped bullets into her husband, Swmbla Basumatary. The president of the All Bodo Students' Union, the powerful student group representing the Bodo ethnic group, died in hospital. It was July 30, 1996. Bhanumati, who was two-and-a-half months pregnant, became a widow.

Unlike Phami, Jaiklong, Khongkar and Dwifang had seen their father and had been growing up under his care. But the cruel jaws of death were waiting to snatch him away. On June 5, 1999, Garla Batha Basumatary, president of the nascent People's Democratic Front, was refuelling his car at a petrol pump in Serfanguri, a highway-side town in Kokrajhar district, when he was shot at from behind by unknown gunmen. After a year of treatment at hospitals in Chennai and Guwahati, Basumatary lost his battle with death. The injuries to his spinal cord, which had been hit by three bullets, proved fatal. He died on September 7, 2000, leaving Raktima a widow. The three boys lost their father.

I met the two widows – Raktima at her sprawling home at Samtaybari, nearly 50 kms north-west of Kokrajahar, and Bhanumati at Salakati, close to Kokrajhar – in early April 2005 and discovered that women who must be both father and mother to their children are forced to lead their households from the front, often battling discrimination by the society around them. If it is a difficult job to run households as women – after overcoming the trauma caused by the untimely death of their husbands – facing life as a widow in conservative rural societies can be challenging.

Widow remarriage is permitted in Bodo society, and widows are not actually discriminated against, but men tend to avoid coming forward to help them for fear of their names being linked to these women.

Raktima was a primary school teacher before her marriage to Garla Batha Basumatary in 1983. Her husband was then secretary of the ABSU's Kokrajhar district unit and headmaster of the Serfanguri High School. A singer and filmmaker of some repute, Basumatary in 1985 made Jariminni Khongkor, the first video film in the Bodo language. In 1990, at the height of the mass uprising

Raktima

for a separate homeland in the Bodo heartland that is spread over the western and northern parts of Assam, he released his audio album, Thwisam. His songs on Bodo nationalism touched the hearts of thousands, and were extremely popular, in keeping with the mood of the time.

The Basumatarys' eldest son Jaiklong, whom the parents lovingly called Raja, was good at his studies, generating much hope in his father's mind. Basumatary was steadily climbing the ladder in the ABSU hierarchy. Life looked settled, and Raktima gave up her job to look after the family full time. In 1993, the ABSU signed a memorandum of understanding (MoU) with the central government, that halted, for a while, the Bodoland uprising. The Bodos were given some amount of autonomy and the Bodoland Autonomous Council (BAC), an elective politico-administrative structure, was formed. Soon, Garla Batha took over as the new president of the ABSU, an organization that was basking in the post-Bodo Accord euphoria.

"Bodo politics was deeply divided. A new rebel group, the Bodo Liberation Tigers had emerged on the scene. My husband, in keeping with his commitment to the Bodo society, wanted to bring about unity among the fragmented Bodo groups and formed the People's Democratic Front on October 26, 1996," Raktima, 39, said, sitting in the porch of her house, overlooking a tree-lined fish pond.

The PDF, which sank into oblivion as quickly as it had emerged, was said to have been aligned to, or was close to, the National Democratic Front of Boroland (NDFB), a rebel group fighting for an independent Bodo nation. Still, Raktima would not like to blame the BLT, the NDFB's arch rival, for her husband's killing. She thinks her husband was a victim of political rivalry and that "certain forces" conspired to take his life. "I don't know why he was killed, but he could, at least, have been given a warning by those who did not like him or his views before they took that extreme step," Raktima said.

She was soon to face life without her husband, and see

its different colours. Raktima did not receive the mandatory ex-gratia payment of Rs. 100,000 from the State Government although her husband was a victim of militants' violence. As though that was not bad enough, she was betrayed by her insurers. "I am still struggling to realize my insurance claim of Rs. 5 lakh from the National Insurance Company which is refusing to part with the money, saying I should have made the claim within three months of the attack on my husband," Raktima said. She has moved the High Court and has spent around Rs. 30,000 fighting the case to get her insurance dues.

"I have been a silent sufferer. I was hoping that the organization that my husband had served for such a long time (he was all along with the ABSU, the PDF stint being very short) would extend some help to me in my hour of crisis. But nobody visited me to enquire as to how I was managing things," Raktima said.

But she was managing all right, thanks to her determination to effectively perform the role of both father and mother to her sons. Jaiklong passed his Class XII examinations securing a first division. Raktima made up her mind to send him to a good college for his bachelor's degree. The young man, currently studying at a Kolkata college, hopes to make it to the Indian Foreign Service.

As far as economic matters go, Raktima is luckier than most widows of violence like her across Assam. Her husband had 42 bighas or about six hectares of land which she has used to the best of her ability to take care of her household and fund her children's education. "I engaged people to cultivate the land in return for half the paddy crop. They could take away the other half. I sell paddy and vegetables at the market in Serfanguri," she said, without a hint of self-consciousness. Raktima was only bothered about her sons' future. She would see that her produce was transported safely to the Serfanguri market from her home at Samtaybari. She would have to negotiate a dirt road with a rickety, and rather dangerous, wooden bridge. At times, she would supervise the sales herself.

What disturbed Raktima and her sons, particularly Jaiklong, the eldest, was the curiosity generated among the people about how the lady was managing to send her sons to pursue their studies outside the area. Her two other sons were pursuing their studies at Guwahati and at a nearby town respectively. She has become somewhat reclusive. She does not socialize much, and visited other people only occasionally, during marriages or to condole a death in a family. But Raktima has charted out the course her sons are to take, a role their father, or both of them, jointly, would have performed under normal circumstances. "They are not going to join politics, or have anything to do with politics, at least while I am alive," Raktima said.

A decade after her husband's death at the hands of suspected NDFB militants, Bhanumati, who managed to get the job of a teacher at the Salakati ME School in 1999, seemed ready to reflect on widowhood. "There is no discrimination as such between men and women in Bodo society. Besides, there is no taboo on widow re-marriage. Still, it is difficult for a man to marry a widow because such a bond usually becomes a point of discussion and curiosity," she said.

Bhanumati is a voracious reader, and loves novels in Bodo, Assamese and Hindi. "I don't mix much with people. Some of them, after all, might think I'm an unlucky woman," she said in a matter-of-fact manner.

If the task of heading a household as a woman, looking after the children, earning a livelihood and ensuring her own security as well as that of her children is in itself a gigantic job, for a widow, managing all of this becomes even more difficult. "A massive awareness programme is needed. A social revolution is necessary in order to remove the doubts and suspicions that confront widows like us," Bhanumati said. Groups like the All Bodo Women's Welfare Federation (ABWWF), she thinks, can do a lot in this direction once it is clear in its objectives. "I myself want to do something for the welfare of widows of violence in my area, but my foremost priority is to look after my daughter and fill the void in her life caused by the death of her father," she said.

Bhanumati is fortunate to have received the ex-gratia payment of Rs. 100,000 from the erstwhile Bodoland Autonomous Council authorities and an equal amount later from the Bodoland Territorial Council (the BAC was dissolved and a new structure called the BTC came up after the new Bodo Agreement signed by the Bodo leaders and New Delhi in 2003). But it was only through her relentless efforts that she was able to get her dues.

"I faced and overcame most of the hurdles by myself. Even the job I got three years after my husband's death was through my own initiative. I feel there should be a mechanism in place to make things a bit easier for people like me who have lost the breadwinners of their families to militant violence," Bhanumati said. Society, she said, should lend its moral support to such women, and not discriminate against them. Otherwise, people such as Raktima and Bhanumati would become recluses, and could lose their will to live. That would hit little children like Phami very hard, and shatter the dreams of people like Jaiklong who have just stepped into adulthood.

Chapter VIII

THE LOSS OF THEIR HUSBANDS TURNED THEM INTO WOMEN OF STEEL

Wives of powerful men are not always women of steel. More often than not, they are simple home-makers, who usually live in their husbands' shadows, but contribute tremendously to their success by keeping them on the right track. Often, these women carry on with their duties selflessly, and remain unsung.

Basanti Sharma

But when they lose their husbands, particularly to trigger-happy militants in violent insurgency theatres like Assam, for instance, they transform themselves into women of steel. There is no looking back for them then as they surge ahead trying to fulfil their husbands' missions in life, and establishing and strengthening their individual identities too, in the process.

Here is the story of three women in Assam, all wives of powerful politicians, whose lives were cut short by insurgents seeking a "homeland" for their people. All of them have gone on to prove that with courage, determination, and a bit of luck, women can take charge of their lives, bring up children as single parents and excel in the fields of their choice. These are examples of the manner in which some of these women lost their husbands, and the way in which they took charge of their lives after that.

February 22, 1991. Manabendra Sharma, General Secretary of the Assam Congress and a top trade union leader, came out of his house in Guwahati's Uzan Bazar locality quite early in the morning. He was on his way to the market nearby. Suddenly, a motorcycle rushed onto the scene and the youths riding it pumped bullets into Sharma. It was 6.45 in the morning. There were people in the area. But, as family members told me later, no voice was raised, and whoever had opened their shops, immediately downed shutters. Manabendra Sharma was dead.

When Manabendra Sharma was shot dead that wintry morning in the heart of Guwahati, his wife Basanti could not weep. "My sons had suddenly lost their father and my mother-in-law her eldest son. I had to keep my shock and grief all to myself for their sake. It was terrible," Basanti Sharma told me at her home in Guwahati.

At once, this schoolteacher was saddled with the responsibility of keeping her two grown up sons on track. The elder one was pursuing his studies for a BA degree, while the younger one was a higher secondary student. Little did Basanti know that fate had willed her to enter the arena of politics. "I never had much interest in politics and I never allowed my husband to bring politics home," she said.

She had been to Parliament just once earlier, to witness the proceedings on a trip that had been organized by former Union Law Minister Dinesh Goswami, a leader from Assam. And here she was, on the verge of plunging into active politics herself. Assam Congress leader Hiteswar Saikia persuaded her to go to the Rajya Sabha as an MP. Basanti Sharma became an MP in 1991 itself and went on to get a second term that ended in 2002.

She took three years to come to terms with the reality of heading the household in the absence of her husband. "My sons were in Guwahati, and I used to come home quite frequently from Delhi. I had to tackle many problems. There were many who used to provoke my sons, pointing out people who they said had killed their father," she said.

Basanti Sharma may have succeeded in successfully steering her sons (the elder went on to become Assam Youth Congress president and later settled down with businesses of his own, and the younger son is also a businessman), but as an MP, and then, as Chairperson of the Assam Women's Commission, she has had to battle the odds in her quest for justice.

"When you have a law in the country, the law should take its own course in delivering justice. But, in my case, it was not so. My husband's killers are still at large," she lamented during my meeting with her in mid-2005. Three people, all militants, were arrested in connection with the killing, but they fled from jail. Two of them later surrendered, while one was killed in a shootout with security forces.

Basanti raised the issue in Parliament, but could not move things. "I failed on this front as an MP," she said. When MPs argued for withdrawal of the Terrorist and Disruptive Activities (Prevention) Act, she was unhappy. That's history, though, and today, Basanti Sharma would not like to rake up old issues. She is, however, bent on delivering justice to the needy women in Assam, particularly the widows of violence. "We are compiling a list of such women who had lost their husbands to violence in the state," she said.

May 6, 1996. Assam Rural Development Minister and State Congress leader Nagen Neog was returning home in his native Baruagaon, 15 kilometres from the District Headquarter town of Golaghat in eastern Assam. He was escorted by security guards who followed him in another vehicle. All of a sudden, militants of the outlawed United Liberation Front of Asom, who were lying in wait, ambushed the two cars at the Singrijan bridge, on the Golaghat-Furkating road. It was 7.45 p.m. It was a very well planned attack, for the militants were said to have intercepted wireless radio

Ajanta Neog

communications from the Minister's motorcade. Neog was killed, along with nine others, eight of whom were security guards, and one, a civilian driver. The rebels decamped with the weapons carried by the security personnel.

Like any other woman, Ajanta Neog, then a housewife, was haunted by a tremendous feeling of insecurity after her husband Nagen Neog was slain by insurgents in a most daring manner. Her sons were very young – ten and five – and she had no separate identity of her own. Moreover, an insensitive state administration had decided to withdraw the house guards and security cover provided to her husband, a senior minister, within twenty four hours of his death.

"The first issue that I had to tackle was that of survival. I concluded that my first priority was going to be my sons. I was prepared to fight all odds to make sure that they lead their lives in a secure and meaningful manner," Ajanta Neog, Minister of State for PWD, told me in early June 2005 at her plush office at the State Secretariat in Guwahati.

This woman was not prepared to leave her husband's wishes unfulfilled. Within two months of the tragedy, she joined the Bar at the Gauhati High Court and enrolled herself for a Master's degree in Law. "The family and the people of my husband's constituency in Golaghat were with me, lending me moral support. I had to be with them as they had always been with my husband," she said.

For that, an individual identity was most important. "By becoming a practicing lawyer, I got a certain identity of my own. The livelihood aspect was also taken care of. And joining the Master's course in Law kept me busy, and also helped to keep my mind occupied," Ajanta Neog said about the recovery phase in her life. She had by then sent off her sons to boarding school.

But she was bent on avenging the death of her husband, though in a different manner. "I decided that the method I was going to choose would be through social work, and politics was the vehicle that would help me achieve my objective," she said. The Congress party obliged her by giving her the party nomination in 2001. Ajanta Neog won the seat held earlier by her husband. Today, she wants the state administration to lay down a mechanism to provide for the security and rehabilitation of women survivors of violence in Assam at different levels.

February 27, 2000. Nagen Sharma, State Forest and Public Works Minister and a top leader of the Asom Gana Parishad, was going for a meeting at the Dakshin Nalbari College, around 5 kilometres from the District Headquarter town of Nalbari in Western Assam. His motorcade came under a bomb attack, which killed him and four others, including his Personal Security Officer.

Alaka Sarma

AGP leader Nagen Sarma's wife Alaka could not believe that her husband had died in a bomb attack when friends from Mumbai reached her in Guwahati by telephone to express their condolences. She first heard of his killing from them, for though she was in Guwahati at that time, nobody around her had plucked up the courage to tell her about it till then. "Nalbari, after all, was my husband's constituency. How could he have been killed there?" she thought. But soon she realized that her husband was no more, and had left her and their ten-year-old daughter.

But this economist, a follower of Jaiprakash Narayan, was not prepared to run away from her duties and the responsibilities that suddenly fell on her shoulders. "My husband was everything to me. The question at that point in time (when he was killed) was whether to return to Mumbai, where I had been based earlier. Besides, my relatives were pleading with me to join them abroad," Alaka told me at her home in Guwahati.

She decided to remain in Assam, and moreover, she made up her mind to enter public life in order to address various issues. Some of the causes and issues dear to her are ensuring justice to the poor within the existing system, people's empowerment and ensuring that such empowerment reaches the lowermost rungs of society, and increasing the productive capacity of Assam's economy.

Alaka said she has "forgiven" her husband's killers, but admitted that insurgency has been retarding the state's growth. "The political class doesn't have any clear concept and neither does it have any definite commitment towards solving the problem of insurgency in Assam. Poor governance and lack of political leadership and direction have sustained insurgency," she observed.

Ever since her husband's death, Alaka has been heading the Nagen Sarma Memorial Society, a non-profit body engaged in social work. Asked what she would like to do for women survivors of violence in Assam given a chance, she listed the following: documentation of such women, an outreach programme to meet such women with "wounded hearts," set up a non-political public forum where all shades of people could pour out their anguish, organize small groups of people for resource awareness, campaign for good governance and draw up a massive economic reconstruction programme.

Alaka may have a long wish list, but she too agrees that there is an urgent need for an institutional response mechanism within the State Government to deal with women survivors of violence across Assam. "Nobody in the Government seems to have a clue about how to deal with such people. Things cannot go on like this for ever," Alaka said. Civil society's role in the state, she said, has been negligible so far in giving succour to women who have lost their husbands or sons in the course of various conflicts within the state. This needs to change.

Alaka contested the by-election (as an AGP candidate) within a month of her husband's death and won the seat, defeating veteran Congressman Bhumidhar Barman. In the very next election, in May 2001, she lost by 10,000 votes. Perhaps Alaka was not familiar with the "political language." Today, however, she is very different, and is moving ahead with a promise to change the lives of at least some people in Nalbari.

Nagen Sarma's death, after all, has drastically changed her own.

Chapter IX

TRAVAILS OF A POLICE OFFICER'S WIFE

October 12, 1990. It was office as usual for Sub-Inspector Dulal Borkotoky, 52, working for the intelligence wing of the Assam Police, called the Special Branch. Duliajan, in eastern Assam's Dibrugarh district, where he was posted, is the field headquarters of the public sector Oil India Limited. But that was not

Amiya Borkotoky

what this sleepy township was famous for in those days. The place, 500 kilometres east of Guwahati, was the hub of the outlawed ULFA, fighting for an independent Assam. It was soon discovered that the deep jungles of Lakhipathar, near Duliajan, where Borkotoky carried out his day-to-day job of gathering intelligence, was the General Headquarters of the ULFA.

Duliajan is a small pot-holed town, and every important address is located within a 3 to 4 kilometre radius. Borkotoky got back home to the OIL campus (he was staying in an OIL accommodation) at 2 p.m. for lunch. He wanted to have the day's meal with his mother who had come to his house two days ago from Borhapjan, near the district town of Tinsukia, not far away. Borhapjan was where Borkotoky hailed from. Lunch over, he returned to office. It was five in the evening when he finished his day's work and headed back home. His wife and mother were already dressed up for an outing when Borkotoky reached his residence. They returned by 7 p.m. After a bath, Borkotoky rested. His mother sat in the living room.

It was close to 8 p.m. A car slowed down and stopped outside Borkotoky's home. "Two men came in and asked our daughter Geetanjali if deuta (father) was around. She said he was in. They sat down. My son suspected them to be ULFA boys and hid his father in the bathroom. The boys said their "sir" wanted to meet him (Borkotoky). A third man had entered by then, carrying a sten gun. My husband eventually came out to meet them. He was shivering with fear," Borkotoky's wife Amiya told me at her home in July 2005 in Jorhat, where the family currently lives. He was asked to get dressed quickly and come with them.

"I fell at their feet, urging them not to take my husband away. The boys replied in a matter-of-fact manner that their group doesn't kill or harm Assamese people. Saying they would return him to us, the men took my husband and drove away," Amiya recalled. She, along with daughter Geetanjali, then a BA Part I student, and son Abhijeet, then in Class XII, had every reason to doubt the words of the abductors. The situation in the state was bad as the armed activities of the ULFA were at their peak. On October 9, 1990, three days before Borkotoky's kidnapping, the rebels had abducted another Assam Police intelligence officer, Giasuddin Ahmed. He had been was picked up from Digboi, not far from Duliajan.

"We huddled together and began to pray. Around 1 a.m. the boys came again. I opened the door. They barged in and wanted me to open the cupboard. I obliged. They immediately started looking through some files that were inside. Before leaving with the files, they told my daughter not to worry, saying her father would be back in about five days or so. They asked us not to inform the police and also told us to maintain that Borkotoky was on leave," Amiya said. From around the third day, policemen started visiting their home, making enquiries about Borkotoky. Amiya kept telling them that he was on leave. Police enquiries gained momentum after a week.

Six months passed. As is normal in such cases, rumours began to do the rounds. Some rumours had it that he had been taken to Delhi by the ULFA and that the group would hold him permanently and utilise his services. Another rumour was that Borkotoky had suffered a heart attack.

March, 1991. One day, the Duliajan police station received a phone call saying Borkotoky was on his way back. Around that time, a cycle-borne youth delivered a letter at his Borhapjan home. Addressed to the "Borkotoky family," the letter said that they had been about to return him, but Borkotoky had had a cardiac arrest and died. The writers of the letter apologized for his death and said they had carried out Borkotoky's funeral with due honour. The body was never handed over to the family.

Amiya's worst fears had come true. She had been in agony all these months at the Borhapjan home of her husband's family. When she received definite news of her husband's death, Amiya performed the necessary rituals. She then made up her mind to face life, surmount the odds and forge ahead, meeting all the challenges. She, after all, was responsible now for the future of her two young children. They returned to Duliajan. Son Abhijeet's education was disrupted.

Taking the advice of family and friends, Amiya got her daughter married in 1992. Her son-in-law, taking into account Abhijeet's mental state, suggested that the family move in with him and shift to Jorhat. This they did. Abhijeet managed to complete his Commerce degree in 1997.

Amiya did receive an ex-gratia payment of Rs. 100,000 from the Assam Government. But a job eluded both her and her daughter. "The authorities had said I would be given a job. I approached the Special Branch top brass two or three times in Guwahati. But nothing actually materialized," Amiya said.

It is very commonly seen that family members who survive the deaths of men killed by trigger-happy militants in Assam have to run from pillar to post, pleading with the authorities to give them the job that is their due. It is also not uncommon to see that in the end, many of the survivors fail to find a job for themselves with the help of which they can keep their home fires burning. The Government does not as a matter of routine offer its helping hand to many such kin of men gunned down by rebels.

Abhijeet could not bear the sudden loss of his father. "I was angry because we could do nothing although my father was kidnapped and had died while in custody. After all, how could we fight an organization?" he lamented. Over the years, he has matured, and is now a young man. Abhijeet's eighteen-month-old son Rongko keeps his grandmother constant company. Amiya dotes on the little one and tries to forget the darkest hour in her life, the death of her husband, for no particular fault of his. Borkotoky, after all, was a government servant doing a job to earn his living. But, insurgents, most of the time, refuse to see reason. They think they have to use the lethal power of their guns to carry on their struggle.

Snatching up little Rongko, who was trying to get out through the front door, Amiya settled down to continue her story. "He (her husband) was so sincere and disciplined that I keep reminding my children of those traits all the time," she said. Amiya recalled something that could have been Borkotoky's premonition of impending danger. "He used to keep saying that the situation was not good. Then, after his colleague Giasuddin was abducted on October 9, 1990 from Digboi, his office staff used to ask him, "What if you are kidnapped next?" He told me this once when he returned from office," she said.

That apprehension of Borkotoky's colleagues proved to be prophetic. He is no more. But, he has left behind Amiya, Geetanjali and Abhijeet, all of whom have proved themselves to be strong survivors.

Chapter X

THE "SECRET KILLERS" WHO WIDOWED BHARATI

Oalbari is a filthy, pot-holed, district town without any footpaths in western Assam, just about 70 kilometres from the capital Guwahati. The district has always been a hotbed of the dreaded ULFA. Several top leaders of the rebel group, including its elusive "Deputy Commander in Chief," Raju Baruah (whose real name is

Bharati Kalita

Hitesh Kalita), the outfit's one-time publicity chief Mithinga Daimary, currently under detention (real name Deepak Das), and Lohit Deuri, a former ULFA "Commandant" who has now surrendered, all hail from this district. These leaders had either pursued or are still vigorously pursuing the ULFA's violent armed campaign for a "sovereign, socialist Assam."

And if one hails from this district and happens to be Bharati Kalita, sister of ULFA top gun Raju Baruah, it is natural for people to look at her as more than just another ordinary Assamese woman. And when, in 1988, Bharati married Dijen Saloi, a small businessman in Nalbari, something more was added to her family profile – she became the sister-in-law of a much-feared ULFA leader. Dijen's younger brother Tapan Saloi happened to be the "Assistant Commandant" of the rebel group's Nalbari unit. So whether Dijen and Bharati liked it or not, they were known as a couple whose kin were top ranking insurgent leaders.

"Yes, it's a fact that our close relatives have been with the ULFA for a long time. But neither me, nor my husband had anything to do with the rebels or their organisation. We tried our best to lead our own lives," Bharati told me at her modest home in Nalbari's Bishnupur locality on a damp Sunday morning earlier this month. But, like many other women in Assam, who have been indirectly drawn into the vortex of the prevailing conflicts in the state, family ties have cost Bharati very dear, too. She ended up losing her husband in the dead of night one day, shot at home by "secret killers" whose identities still remain a mystery, despite conjectures. Dijen had just turned fifty, when the gunmen cut short his life.

It was January 3, 2001. Owls hooted in the dark night outside. It was 1 a.m. There were still more than three hours left for daybreak. Dijen Saloi, his wife Bharati, their eleven-year-old son Ankur and seven-year-old daughter Barnali, were all sound asleep. Suddenly, the silence of the night was shattered by the roar of car engines. Two vehicles came to a stop in front of their house. "The men knocked at the door, broke it open and barged inside. They first entered the room where my husband's nephew Pulen (son of Dijen's younger brother) was sleeping along with his cousin Arup. The men asked them the whereabouts of our room," Bharati recalled.

Having pinpointed Dijen's room in the joint-family home, seven masked men, all armed and clad in black trousers and jackets, called out, "Bou, (a respectful term for an elder brother's wife) open the door or else we shall force ourselves inside." They broke open the door anyway, and started looking for Dijen. "Soon, they found him hiding under the bed. A gunman pumped bullets into him immediately, killing him. They shot Pulen dead too, and then left," Bharati said, tears rolling down her eyes. Within minutes, the youths returned and sprayed bullets at Arup, injuring him badly. He survived, but still limps from that injury. Both Pulen and Arup were tenth standard students at that time.

On the surface, Dijen and Bharati should have had no cause for worry. In the normal course of events, it would have been assumed that the rebels would not touch them, since they were close relatives of top ULFA leaders. And the security forces, too, would not target them for they had no direct links with the ULFA whatsoever despite being kin of senior rebel leaders. But the dynamics of conflict in Assam, both in the past and today, has been far from simple. A day before Dijen's killing, suspected ULFA rebels had shot Avinash Bordoloi, a surrendered ULFA member at Horihotuli, near the Police Reserve in Nalbari. Avinash had just bid adieu to arms and was planning to settle down to a normal life.

Retaliation for such killings was already in vogue. Mystery killers would target the family members of top ULFA leaders. These were to pass off as "secret killings," implying that either former rebels on their own or with direct or indirect assistance from the men in uniform were behind these attacks ostensibly aimed at sending a message down to the rebels to stop their killing spree. ULFA publicity chief Mithinga Daimary's family members were eliminated by "secret killers." And a month before the fatal attack on Dijen, ULFA "Foreign Secretary" Sasha Choudhury's brother, Deepak, was gunned down by some as yet unidentified men at Helosa, near Sarthebari in Barpeta district.

Bharati said her husband never thought that he or his immediate family could become the target of "anti-ULFA forces." She said: "Of course, my husband always got very worried about the safety of my family who lived at Charia village, near Nalbari. Whenever there was an attack by the ULFA, he would visit Charia and get my sister to live with us for fear of retaliation by certain forces." Dijen's fears were not unfounded: his wife's family was spared, but not his wife. She had to lose him. Dijen was clearly a victim of the peculiar currents and cross-currents of the prevailing conflicts in Assam.

Her husband's death had an immediate and severe impact on Bharati. She had to close down the grocery shop that Dijen had been running for a living. She rented out the premises. Mortgaging the little land the family owned, Bharati started building a small tin-roofed house in the locality where she had spent her married life. Her brother, a schoolteacher, helped her with some money that he gathered by selling off some of his own land. Bharati recalled the day, October 28, 1998, when she joined the job she got: that of a primary schoolteacher at the Debiram Prathamik Vidyalay, not far from where she now lives. "If I had not had this job, my life today would have been even more miserable. How would I have brought up my two children?" she remarked.

What about help from the Government? Hadn't she received the usual ex-gratia payment of Rs. 100,000 that the immediate kin of a person dying in a violent incident is supposed to get from the authorities? Bharati replied: "Some policemen had told me at that time that I would get Rs. 100,000 as ex-gratia provided I made a request in writing and also state that it was the ULFA that had killed my husband. How could I write or state something that is not true? So, I decided not to think of any help from the Government." Bharati was firm in her belief that her husband was not shot by ULFA militants, and always insisted that the ULFA was not involved. This may or may not have been true, but Bharati herself is convinced of it.

Bharati said that despite "moral support" from the society, she actually had to face the struggle all by herself. Aside from the cash crunch, she had to deal with her children's traumas, caused by the killing of their father right in front of their eyes. "I was drifting in and out of consciousness for almost a week after the incident. My son was hit by depression but did not talk much for fear that it might disturb me further. But gradually, he started behaving in a very defiant manner," she said. Even today, Ankur, who is very mature for his age, doesn't seem to trust anyone. The trauma of losing his father for no fault of his no doubt still haunts this young man. Sadly though, he has not received any counselling so far. And his condition is certainly not beyond repair.

Apart from worrying about the future of her children, Bharati is eagerly awaiting justice. "My husband is dead, and so are many other innocent men. All I want now is justice. The authorities must find the killers and punish them," she said. Doesn't she think that all this would not have happened if the ULFA had not come into existence in Assam in the first place? Bharati replied, "If not the ULFA, some other radical youths would perhaps have emerged on the scene in the state. After all, one must look at the reasons for the rise of an armed insurgency. Isn't Assam economically backward? There are no jobs for the youths."

Having said this, Bharati would like the ULFA to try and fulfil its objectives in a peaceful manner, through talks and a "give and take" approach. And yes, she would tell brother Hitesh (ULFA "Deputy Commander in Chief") this, in case she happens to meet him. "It's now more than 15 years since I last saw my brother. It seems impossible to meet him now. But I pray that wherever he is, he remains safe, and that God will look after him," Bharati said, in fond remembrance of her brother.

In his sister's eyes, he is a kid brother first, and a rebel chieftain only later.

Chapter XI

WHY TRIBENI DOESN'T LIKE POLITICIANS ANYMORE...

Tribeni Baruah, popularly known as Rubi, doesn't like politicians anymore. Her children on their part hate black cars. They have reasons for their dislikes. After all not everybody loses their husband or father early in life, that, too, dying at the hands of militants for no fault of their own.

Tribeni Baruah

February 27, 2000. Pranabesh Baruah left his home at Nalbari — around 70 kilometres west of Guwahati — early, without even taking his usual bath, telling wife Tribeni that he would be returning shortly. "I told him to change his clothes, but he was in a hurry. He simply took out his bicycle and left," Tribeni told me at her home in the heart of the decrepit district town on a damp morning in August 2005.

At 59, Baruah had an active lifestyle. After dabbling a bit in business, he had focused on his work as an educationist all his life. Besides, he was dynamic in the field of social work in Nalbari, his home district. He had once taught at the Handique Girls' College, a premier women's college in Guwahati, before joining his wife to set up the Honsons English School near his home in 1994.

"Everybody liked my husband, particularly the youths. Peace was always uppermost on his mind and he used to tell the young people that all their grievances could be solved through peaceful means. Therefore, I never ever imagined that any harm could come to him, particularly from militants or through violence," Tribeni said.

So when Baruah rushed out that morning, no premonition crossed Tribeni's mind. The day was full of engagements for the family: they had a marriage to attend and their two daughters were to present a dance item at a function in a local college. Tribeni was busy until noon, getting her daughters ready for their performance.

"At 12.45 p.m. the phone rang. The caller asked about

the whereabouts of 'Baruah Sir'. A short while later, a guardian of one of our school students telephoned and asked for my husband. The person enquired if I knew that minister Nagen Sharma's car had been bombed," Tribeni recalled.

Even then, she did not think that anything untoward had happened to her husband. It was lunch time. Tribeni and her children decided to go ahead and have their food. By this time, a crowd had gathered in front of their school. Everyone was asking, "Where is Baruah Sir?"

Someone from the crowd said he had seen "Baruah Sir" travelling with minister Nagen Sharma in a black car. That was it. The Baruahs, and the families of four others who were killed that day, will never forget that black February morning.

A family friend of the Baruahs, a doctor, asked Tribeni to get into his car. They drove straight to the Civil Hospital, not far away. "Till that moment, I never really thought my husband was one of the victims of the devastating blast," she said.

But it was at the hospital that Tribeni actually realized that her husband was no more. She was brought home. Tribeni lost consciousness. Her mother-in-law, who was with them, was shattered at the news of her son's death.

Baruah was killed along with four others, including Nagen Sharma, a top leader of the Asom Gana Parishad, a regional party that was in power in Assam at that time. Sharma, who was State Forest and Public Works Minister, was going for a meeting at the Dakshin Nalbari College, around 5 kilometres from Nalbari, when his motorcade came under a bomb attack. The outlawed ULFA, engaged in a violent armed campaign for an independent homeland, was generally blamed for that deadly bomb attack.

Baruah died that day just because he happened to be in the minister's car, travelling with him. "My husband liked Nagen (Sharma) a lot. It was a quirk of fate that he was with him, in the same car, that morning," Tribeni said. She became a widow. So did Nagen Sharma's wife, Alaka, an economist and development activist.

It is a different matter that Alaka later stepped into her husband's shoes by joining politics and becoming an MLA. But Tribeni had to carry on her mission, that of running her school and bringing up her three children, son Simanta, and daughters Indrani and Darshana.

It isn't surprising that Tribeni has started disliking politicians after that tragic incident, all the more so after the then Chief Minister Prafulla Kumar Mahanta, who was Nagen Sharma's colleague, apparently ignored her plea for help. "Mahanta visited me at my Nalbari home after the incident and offered his condolences. Later, I went to see him, accompanied by Alaka (Nagen Sharma's wife), and presented him with a memorandum requesting some assistance for my school," Tribeni recalled.

The Chief Minister did promise to consider, but according to Tribeni, did nothing after that. "I met Chandra

Mohan Patowari (another senior AGP leader) also. The only AGP leader from whom I got some support for the school was Rekharani Das Boro, who gave me fifty thousand rupees," she said.

It was then that Tribeni decided not to seek the help of anyone in the Government any more. "Abruptly, I thought, why should I beg? I gave up the attempts and began to generate resources on my own to run the school that was my husband's passion," she said.

Apart from running the school, Tribeni had to counsel her children at home. "My children turned a little aggressive. My daughters developed a revulsion for black cars as their father had been riding one such on that fateful day. Besides, they began to hate politicians and ministers, and would either switch off or change channels on TV if any minister appeared in the programme," she said.

Such behaviour could have been the symptoms of some sort of post-traumatic stress disorder as the children were directly impacted by the death of their father. Only those who lose their loved ones all of a sudden, caught in the vortex of mindless violence, can possibly realize the extent of the trauma.

If Tribeni lost her husband, the political establishment of the time has lost her sympathy. There are not many examples in insurgency-ravaged states such as Assam, of the state authorities, including the political leadership, dealing with a survivor with sensitivity.

If many of the poor women survivors across the state were made to run around before they were paid the ex-gratia amount of Rs. 100,000 (the next-of-kin of anyone killed in militancy-related incidents was paid that amount), the authorities antagonized comparatively better-off people like Tribeni by their insensitivity to their feelings. For instance, Chief Minister Mahanta could have easily organized some financial assistance, irrespective of the amount, for Tribeni's school at Nalbari.

Most survivors, however, do receive some kind of support, even if it is just moral support, from other quarters. In Tribeni's case, local youths from Nalbari visited her and tried to give her solace. "I don't know if any ULFA members were among those who visited me in my hour of crisis. But what touched me was that they profusely apologized for my husband's death," she said.

Today, Tribeni sees herself as a peace activist and social worker. However, she will not use politics to achieve her objectives. "I do not really hate the ULFA as they must have had some reason to take up arms. But if I do happen to meet its leaders, I will try to convince them to resolve their problems in a peaceful manner," she said.

After her husband's death in a rebel bomb attack, Tribeni has started looking at the problem of militancy more closely, developing, in the process, strong views on the matter. "Poor governance and rise of militancy are inter-related. Joblessness and lack of opportunities have forced many young boys to join militant groups," she said.

Ask her whether she hopes for an early solution to the militancy problem in Assam, and Tribeni gets agitated. "The politicians themselves do not want a solution to the problem of militancy in the state. They have their own selfish motives," she remarked.

If, as Tribeni thinks, it is poor governance that is among the causes of militancy in economically under-developed states like Assam, lack of sensitivity in handling survivors has distanced a large number of them from the government.

But then the authorities have never really responded to the different dimensions of the conflict in a holistic manner. Instead, they are known for the ad hoc measures that they take when confronted with a crisis.

Chapter XII

EVEN A REBEL CHIEFTAIN'S MOTHER WEEPS

She's like any other grandmother anywhere on earth — affectionate, wise and caring. But sorrow engulfs Miliki Baruah, 78. After all, she has lost one son to the bullets of unknown gunmen, and another, although alive, has been away from home for as long as 25 years.

Sadness, however, cannot overpower this highly

Miliki Baruah

focused woman who has clear views of her own. She has been quite forcefully calling for an end to the bloodshed in her native Assam even as her elusive son Paresh Baruah, "Commander in Chief" of the outlawed United Liberation Front of Asom, continues to lead his group's violent "homeland" campaign.

Miliki's life has had its own share of ups and downs, much like anyone else's. Married to Dwijen Baruah, a farmer in the village of Jerai Chokoliboria, near the eastern district town of Dibrugarh, she became the mother of five sons and a daughter.

Life was just fine at Jerai, a village of around 20,000 people, mostly belonging to the Motok, Ahom, tea and ex-tea garden communities with a sprinkling of Muslims. Later, Jerai Chokoliboria was to become famous as the village which three top ULFA leaders called home. These were ULFA's military chief Paresh Baruah, its "General Secretary" Golap Baruah aka Anup Chetia, and Chakra Gohain, one-time "Deputy Commander in Chief" who has now surrendered.

At one time, though, the village was known for its star footballers such as Rebati Phukan, who is now among those named by the ULFA in early September 2005 to explore peace with New Delhi. It is like countless other villages in Assam, surrounded by thick bamboo groves and areca nut trees. The residents are simple people, but conscious and aware of the prevailing situation in the state.

Things were moving fine for Miliki and Dwijen Baruah.

Eldest son Bimal got a job at the Army Supply Depot in the nearby town of Panitola. Second son Pradip was employed with the Military Engineering Service. Third son Paresh Baruah, who had made a name for himself as a fine footballer and volleyball player, had secured employment with the Railways, and was posted at Tinsukia. While her fourth son Dinesh followed Paresh, also joining the Railways, youngest son Bikul became a teacher at a local school.

Life began to change for the Baruahs sometime around 1979-80 when Paresh, who was staying at a Railways Mess in Tinsukia, disappeared. Ever since, he has continued to be in the limelight as the dreaded military boss of the ULFA, a group they formed on April 7, 1979, to achieve a "sovereign, socialist Assam." Jerai Chokoliboria became the favourite destination of the police, the Army and the paramilitary, all wanting information about the local boy who had turned into a dreaded guerrilla chieftain.

For the next fifteen years, the Baruah family, like many others at Jerai, became victims of a familiar cat-and-mouse game. They had started getting used to the midnight knock by men in uniform. Everyone knew Paresh was unlikely to be home, but then psychological pressure, after all, is a common anti-insurgency practice.

On a cold winter night – February 19, 1994 – two cars stopped in front of Rebati Phukan's house at Jerai. Some men disembarked and, after a while, drove away with Dinesh, who was there at that time. The next day, his body was found lying by the National Highway, near Chabua, riddled with bullets. Family ties had cost the Baruahs dear. The killers were not known, but clearly it was a kind of revenge attack. Korobi became a widow. She had been married to Dinesh for just seven months.

The family received me warmly when I visited their spacious tin-roofed house at Jerai on an April morning in 2005. As I scanned the living room, I noticed a name-plate that said "D.Baruah, NFR" (Northeast Frontier Railway). It was a memento, constantly reminding the Baruah family of one of its lost sons. Korobi was not there either, for she had left for her parents' home.

Bimal, the eldest of the brothers, talked quite frankly. "We had all gone through tremendous mental agony during 1984-85. The security personnel visited us for searches and questionings regularly and things were difficult," he said. He remembered younger brother Paresh as a bright student who had received recognition for merit at the lower primary stage.

A brown shawl wrapped around her body, bespectacled Miliki joins us in the conversation. "People are now saying the boys (ULFA cadres) must start peace talks with the Government. But these people must do something concrete and not just harp on the need for talks," she began.

Miliki, flanked by son Bikul and daughter-in-law Renu, added: "There's no point beating about the bush. Everyone –

the ministers, central leaders and the people – must work together to bring peace back to Assam. But at the same time, there is a need to know why the boys (the ULFA activists) are leading such a difficult life, staying in the jungles, braving the sun and the rain."

I met Miliki and two of her sons a couple of months before the ULFA, in early September, nominated an 11 member panel, calling it the People's Consultative Group, to begin preparatory talks with New Delhi and set the ground for possible direct talks between the rebel leadership and the Centre. Award winning Assamese novelist Dr Indira Goswami, popularly known as Mamoni Raisom, was very much on the scene already, having been formally accepted by the ULFA to act as a facilitator, to try and bring the two warring sides together for peace talks.

Miliki said: "If a woman (Mamoni Raisom) can come forward to facilitate the return of peace in Assam, why are the other big guns not doing so?" Obviously, she as a mother is yearning to get her elusive son Paresh back even while trying to overcome the tragedy of losing Dinesh.

"I could do nothing. My son was killed… Only a mother can understand the pangs of losing one's son. Dinesh had never done anything wrong; he was busy pursuing his passion, playing football. He (Dinesh) could not kill even a pigeon," she said.

Today, Miliki, despite being ULFA boss Paresh Baruah's mother, is seen by many as a crusader for peace in the strife-torn state. Her views and comments get adequate media coverage. "Lots of mothers across Assam have lost their sons. Boys, belonging both to the ULFA and the security forces, are still dying. I can't understand why the Government is not really bothered. I would like the killings to stop and the two sides should call a truce and talk peace," Miliki said.

In homes across Assam, there are many parents like Miliki who have been caught in the crossfire just because of family ties – a son being with the ULFA and other children working for the Government, the Public sector or even the Army, police or the paramilitary. There have been instances where the family members of rebel cadres have been tortured by the security forces. Such actions have only strengthened the resolve of the rebels.

In fact, people like Miliki should be regarded as peace-makers and treated as such. Unfortunately, the law-enforcing agencies tend to go by conventional anti-insurgency methods which can never cure the problem, and in the long run turns counter-productive.

Look at this, for instance: on November 5, 2000, unknown gunmen fired three rounds at the house in Jerai where Miliki and the others stay. Again, in 2003, around 50 to 60 rounds were fired at the same house from automatic rifles. The assailants fled when security guards posted at the house by the State Government fired back. These attacks, although unsuccessful, were obviously not casual raids by miscreants.

As the efforts for peace initiated by Dr Indira Goswami gathered momentum by October 2005, the women in the Baruahs' home at Jerai hoped for a peaceful future when they could all lead a normal life. "We only hope we can get a better, peaceful tomorrow, a tomorrow where Assam will shine," Bikul's wife, Renu, said.

The men too are clamouring for peace. "We do not want killings, either by the militants or from the Government's side. Enough blood has been shed already," said Bimal. His brother Bikul added: "We want peace talks, we are with the people."

On her part, Miliki is constantly worried about her son Paresh's safety. "The fire will always burn inside me till I die. I shall continue to wait for Paresh till my last breath. I want him to return home," were her final words to me.

Epilogue

A common sight greeted me at the homes of each of the women I visited while I was working on this series — a framed photograph of the dead husband. These women may be heading their households after the lives of their husbands were cut short, but they still appear to be living in their shadows. Most of these women received me warmly and, contrary to my expectations, did not hesitate to speak about the tragedies that had shattered their lives. But inevitably, as we spoke, each one of them broke down. If the tears were an expression of their sadness and trauma, their composure the very next moment showed their determination to face life and move ahead.

If their tragedies are similar, so are their stories of survival. Tillottama Basumatary became a widow when her husband fell to the bullets of rebels while he was at the market one morning. Kamrun Nissa's husband was gunned down by masked men outside his home as he was playing with his son. Anita Mashahary and Janaki Brahma lost their husbands after they were kidnapped and killed, and Lakshi and Jashmi Hembrom's husbands were victims of a deadly ethnic riot.

Similarly, Bharati Rajkonwari's husband was shot and killed at point-blank range as he stood outside his office. Gunmen barged into Bharati Kalita's home and shot her husband dead under the bed where he was hiding. Amiya Borkotoky's husband, a policeman, was kidnapped and killed. Hemoprova Konwar faced the horror of gunmen pumping bullets into her husband right on the verandah of her house one dark night. And Ajanta Neog, Alaka Sharma and Basanti Sharma became widows because their politician husbands were shot dead or bombed by insurgents.

From the Bodo tribal heartland of Kokrajhar in western Assam to the district of nearby Nalbari, going right up to the districts of Dibrugarh and Tinsukia in the extreme east, violence has touched people, impacting severely on their lives. The survivors, whose stories I have detailed, belong to a wide spectrum of society: wives of schoolteachers, student and political leaders, of close relatives of militant bosses, of daily wage earners, police officers and PSU employees and small businessmen.

While women like Tillottama lost their husbands in random attacks by militants out to "prove their strength," others, like the husbands of Anita and Janaki, were selectively picked up because of their role as student leaders, becoming victims of murky local politics. The two Bharatis, Bharati Rajkonwari and Bharati Kalita, lost their husbands because of their family ties. While Bharati Rajkonwari's husband was the brother of Arabinda Rajkhowa, "Chairman" of the dreaded ULFA, Bharati Kalita is the sister of ULFA's elusive "Deputy Commander in Chief," Raju Baruah. Their husbands were killed by people who could have been "secret killers," a mystery gang I have talked about earlier.

Lakshi and Jashmi became widows because their husbands got caught in the bloody Bodo-Santhal ethnic riots that had swept the western Assam Bodo belt in 1996, and later in 1998. Both Adivasis, their husbands were killed by marauding miscreants belonging to the Bodo community. And Ajanta, Alaka and Basanti are the survivors of political killings. Ajanta's husband was a Congress Minister who was killed while travelling in a car. Similarly, Alaka's husband Nagen Sharma, a Minister belonging to the Asom Gana Parishad was bombed while he was travelling in his car to a meeting. Basanti's husband, Manabendra Sharma, a senior Congress leader, was shot dead near his home when he was going to the market.

It has been proved that anybody can become a victim of violence in a volatile theatre of insurgency and ethnic turf wars. An innocent person just out shopping in the village marketplace gets killed; so do relatives of top rebel leaders. If on one occasion ULFA hit squads had chased and killed a Superintendent of Police in Assam, at other times the brothers of the ULFA's topmost duo, "Chairman" Rajkhowa and "Commander in Chief" Paresh Barua, were murdered in cold blood. The impact of such killings is being felt directly by the wives, children and parents of such victims.

The widows of violence speak the same language, irrespective of whether they are kin ULFA militants, or are wives of police officers, politicians or ordinary citizens. This is the language of deep anguish, pain, trauma and hardship. All of them talk constantly about the need for peace. Moreover, in the initial stages after losing their husbands, who were usually the main breadwinners of the family, they had all been hit by the fear of the unknown, and the insecurity of facing an uncertain future. Besides, the responsibility of bringing up the children and managing the household weighed heavily on them.

It was seen that neither the government nor the society has been really sensitive to these women survivors. This is contrary to the prevalent view that the society comes forward to help such survivors cope with their tragedies and rebuild their lives. Anita, for instance, related how her neighbours in the village would not visit her house for fear that the killers could target them for coming to her aid. And the worst was the shunning of widows by Bodo men for fear that their names could be linked to such women, with negative social consequences.

The Government on its part has no institutionalized response mechanism, nor any specific rules laid down to deal with the widows of violence. As a result, the survivors had to make dozens of visits to the local Deputy Commissioner's office to get the mandatory ex-gratia payment of Rs. 100,000 payable to victims of violence. Surprisingly, till recently, the authorities were paying the ex-gratia amount in cash, and that perhaps is the reason why some of the survivors said they had not received the full amount. The clerks or even officials could actually keep Rs. 30,000 aside from the ex-gratia amount due to each of the recipients. Later, following complaints, the authorities started making ex-gratia payments by cheques, causing much inconvenience to many of the survivors from rural areas who do not have access to banks or bank accounts in their name. Moreover, there is no procedure laid down for providing employment to women who have lost their husbands to insurgency or ethnic strife. One expects such rules to be in place in a state like Assam since it has been in the grip of violence for more than two decades at a stretch.

Despite the odds, these women have shown remarkable courage and determination in overcoming the crises, taking charge of their households and moving ahead in life. Most of them said they had decided to forget the past and hide their grief for the sake of their children. Bringing up their children has been the most important challenge for most of these women.

One common refrain among all the survivors has been their aversion to the idea of revenge. Rather, many, including Miliki Baruah, mother of ULFA "Commander in Chief" Paresh Baruah, said she would like peace to return to Assam. This, despite the fact that one of her sons was gunned down by unknown killers.

However, some of the women I met said they would not like to take the lead in organizing the survivors of violence and lobby for their rights and so on. Many said they have lost faith in both the society and the government. Many simply wanted to be left alone. Of course, others like Bharati Rajkonwari were keen on forming an organization to look after the widows of violence. And women such as Ajanta, a Minister, and Alaka, another political leader, were eager to go all out and do what they could to help the widows of violence, through an established governmental mechanism.

My series was aimed at trying to bring the stories of these women survivors to the people. From this point on, it is up to civil society, the government and the non-governmental agencies or groups to try and work for these survivors and make their lives a little easier. What surprised me was the discovery that neither the government nor civil society works with any definite plan or guidelines to help these women in distress.

If these women are surviving today, it is because they are determined not to succumb to adversity. Most significantly, they had themselves found the strength and the means, however feeble, to rehabilitate themselves. Tillottama, for instance, managed to get her family pension four years after her husband's death, and that too, after doing the rounds of government offices dozens of times. And her son Milon took three years to secure the job of a primary schoolteacher. He got the job not because he was listed as a "martyr's" son, but because he was persistent in his efforts.

Similarly, Hemoprova Konwar never got a government job although she had approached the then Assam Chief Minister. And it was not easy for her to get employment with the Hindustan Fertiliser Corporation where her husband had worked. If she did finally secure the job of a primary schoolteacher at an HFC-run school, it was because of the pressure and efforts of the employees' union of the Corporation.

By the mid-nineties, killings and counter-killings had become common across Assam. The number of widows was on the rise. Perhaps the authorities decided to take the easy way out by not doing anything for such survivors, except paying the ex-gratia amount of Rs. 100,000, which was later raised to Rs. 300,000. There is more than one example of such treatment given to a widow of violence in my series.

Providing a means of livelihood is one aspect. Another is making a systematic effort to give mental succour to the survivors. It is indeed strange that although Assam has been in the grip of insurgent violence and ethnic strife since the late eighties, the authorities have not thought it necessary to provide professional counselling to the survivors of violence.

It would be good to see someone actually intervening, making a list of Assam's widows of violence, and then giving them some support. I am certain that this needs to be done in every theatre of conflict, anywhere in the world. The wounded hearts need a healing touch.

Wasbir Hussain is a senior journalist based in Guwahati, northeastern India. He currently writes for *The Sentinel*, Guwahati, *Outlook*, New Delhi, and The Associated Press news wire. Besides, he is Director, Centre for Development & Peace Studies, a Guwahati-based non-profit think-tank, and is an Associate Fellow with the Institute for Conflict Management, New Delhi.

He has been covering insurgency, ethnic strife, and other major political and social developments in the seven northeastern Indian states for the past 21 years. Before his present assignment, Hussain was Consulting Editor, *The Newspaper Today*, India Today Group Online; Editor, *The Northeast Daily*, Guwahati; Special Correspondent with *The Asian Age*; Regional Editor of *The Telegraph*; and Special Correspondent of *The Telegraph*.

He bagged the 1996 Sanskriti Foundation National Award for excellence in journalism. Wasbir lives in Guwahati with wife Seema, daughter Nazia and son Farhan. He can be reached at wasbir@yahoo.com